Secrets of Watchman Nee

A SPIRIT-FILLED CLASSIC

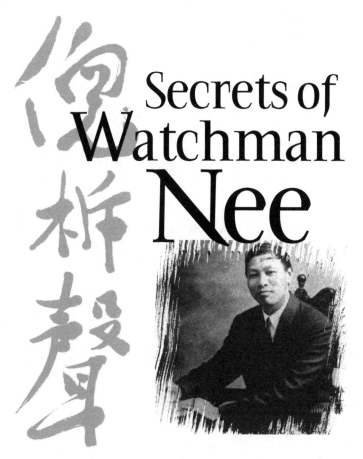

Secrets of Watchman Nee

by Dana Roberts

Bridge-Logos

Orlando, Florida 32822

Bridge-Logos

Orlando, FL 32822 USA

Secrets of Watchman Nee
by Dana Roberts

Library of Congress Catalog Card Number: pending
International Standard Book Number 0-88270-010-3

All scriptures quoted by Watcman Nee are from the American Standard Version. Those quoted by Mr. Roberts are from *The Holy Bible: New International Version*. Copyright 1973, 1978, 1984. International Bible Society.

G163.317.B.m609.35230

Contents

Preface vii

Introduction xiii

1. Watchman Nee and the Work of the Little Flock 1

2. Introduction to Nee's Literature 53

3. The Word and Its Ministry 73

4. Nee's Anthropology: The Spiritual Man and His Life 91

5. The Church and Its Work 147

6. Summary and Conclusions 167

Appendix A 181

Appendix B 185

Bibliography 187

To all my children

Andrew, Jennifer, and Rebecca

Preface

These past few years I have been teaching and studying on Hainan Dao, China. In the Chinese language, Hainan Dao means *South Sea Island*. Like Hawaii, it is a place of pineapples, beauty contests, and tropical beaches. If you look at a map of Asia, you'll see it. It's a few miles south of Mainland China, just east of North Vietnam.

Vietnam Vets know the place. It's on the Gulf of Tonkin. During the war years of the 60s and 70s, we got to see a lot Hainan. It was on the wall just behind Defense Secretary Robert McNamara or President Lyndon Johnson. Hainan made a brief appearance in the 1997 James Bond film *Tomorrow Never Dies*. Then in April of 2001, a midair collision, an emergency landing, and international negotiations made many search their gazetteers for an island the size of Maryland.

I jog through Hainan University. I plug my ears into Mp3's of Watchman Nee's *The Normal Christian Life*, Felix Mendelssohn's *Violin Concerto in E Minor*, and Bible studies by a Baptist teacher named Tony Campolo. I've read *The Normal Christian Life* many times. Mr. Campolo speaks about the Biblical Year of Jubilee. Yet, this particular day it is the Jewish Christian composer who moves me most. Mendelssohn speaks without words. I can hear the joy, the laughter, and the suffering common to all believers. Only the children of Adam have the gift of music. Only we can hear and understand the wide range of passion in this concerto. I stop running and walk along a street shaded by two rows of Magnolia trees. The trees, the music, the preaching conclude my run in breathless devotion and praise.

I rarely hug trees. They're the finger craft of God. Each day I see something more wondrous: people. We're fallen humanity and yet just below the angels (Heb. 2:9). God didn't sprout leaves and branches. He fashioned himself with limbs and fingers like us all. Along my street, I see the Communist Party leader, the graduate law student, the garbage picker, and the homeless lady dressed in filthy rags. All are all embraced by God on the cross. God's greatest gift is offered to them all.

Mendelssohn's wordless message directs the eyes to see them from a spiritual point of view (2 Cor. 5:16). Another day's inspiration might come from a farmer sowing seeds, reading a book, listening to a sermon, or remembering old friend's imitating Christ. The story of God's love in Christ cannot be entirely contained in images of seeds, field lilies, a bride, and a bridegroom, or in the sounds of a lifetime of sermons. It is defined in one great book, the Holy Bible. It is contained and composed in the life, death, and resurrection of Our Lord and Savior. John says, "Jesus did many other things as well. If every one of them were written down, I suppose that even the whole world would not have room for the books that would be written" (John 21:25). The pages of these books are our life in Christ.

This is a small book about one Chinese Christian and his ideas. It is intended to be critical without being destructive. We live in an age where a critical, destructive spirit has been unleashed again. Michael Moore's films, such as *Fahrenheit 911*, the speeches of anarchists Howard Zinn and Norm Chomsky are popular among the young Internet generation.*

---

* Michael Moore is well known for his films *Fahrenheit 9/11* (2004) and *Bowling for Columbine* (2002). The lectures of Noam Chomsky and Howard Zinn demonize the U. S. government and large corporations and play on our fears of the word "big." Their flamboyant styles are like those of religious demogogues or Senator Joseph P. McCarthy in the early 1950s. The opinion is more important than the facts.

More than skeptics, they are cynics. It's a perilous attitude. Cynicism, not skepticism, is at war with God's grace and civilization. In the twenty-first century, a cynical spirit among the saints is common. Jesus knew our hearts all too well. He prayed for the Spiritual unity of all believers (John 17:20-23). This is not the time to divide the church with destructive criticism. For the past two thousand years, the unity of the church, with its constructive criticism, has drawn people to Christ. When people see God's children dwelling together in peace and love, then they are willing to live there, too. If we continue in name-calling and disunity devoid of the Spirit, they may close the church doors and walk away.

The poet and literary scholar, Matthew Arnold (1822-1888), has good advice for Christian writers and preachers. The job of the constructive critic is to "to learn and propagate the best that is known."* Arnold's idea is to first analyze what makes for great literature and then see if those elements are present or absent in other works. The Bible says we ought to do the same (Philippians 4:8-9; 1 Thessalonians 5:19-20). The Christian critic's job is to learn and propagate all that is good and true about God. The critic reviews other writings to uncover the good that is and isn't there. It is the way of Priscilla and Aquila in the Book of Acts:

> Meanwhile a Jew named Apollos, a native of Alexandria, came to Ephesus. He was a learned man, with a thorough knowledge of the Scriptures. He had been instructed in the way of the Lord, and he spoke with great fervor and taught about Jesus accurately, though he knew only the baptism of John. He began to speak boldly in the synagogue. When Priscilla and Aquila heard him, they invited him to their home and explained to him the way of God more adequately (Acts 18:24-26).

---

* Arnold, Matthew. *The Function of Criticism at the Present Time* (London and Cambridge: MacMillan and Co., 1865) p. 23.

Of course, Christians make mistakes. Abraham, Moses, and David slipped up. Even Peter had failings as a Christian leader. We all make errors. Sometimes we make Christianity too American or too Chinese. When we do, we make God and the Gospel less glorious. Constructive criticism is our ally, not our enemy. It's hard on our souls to test our own thoughts and feelings with that of Scripture and the Holy Spirit. Harder still to grow without it.

A word of thanks is offered to the people who helped me to write both the first and second editions of this book. This study was accomplished through the aid of other brothers in Christ to whom thanks are gratefully given here. First to Dr. Harvey J.S. Blaney, who first encouraged me to write a master's dissertation on Nee. Warmest thanks are given to the faculty of Eastern Nazarene College, especially Drs. Wilbur H. Mullen, Albert L. Truesdale and Alvin H. Kauffman for guiding me in the preparation of the first edition. In addition I would like to thank those who advised me in my research: The Rev. Edwin Stube; Rev. Freedom Wentworth II, Drs. Douglas Stuart and Roger R. Nicole, librarian Robert Dvorak and his associate, Kenneth Umenhofer, all from the faculty of Gordon-Conwell Theological Seminary; Rev. W.H. Holton of the Alliance Bible Seminary on Cheung Chaus Island, Hong Kong; Dr. Charles W. Carter of the China Evangelical Seminary in Taipei, Taiwan; and Dr. A. Donald Fredlund of Christian Literature Crusade. I would also like to thank Mr. Wing-Tai Leung, Miss Joyce Leung, and Mr. Cheng Man-lung for translating and making available certain Chinese sources. I wish to also thank the staff of Logos Haven Books for their editorial assistance. Special thanks to Drew Thomas and Beverly Browning and their gifts of encouragement. Thanks go to my entire family for their patience during the writing of the first and second editions of this book.

Finally, there's one more "thanks" to give. I did not meet Watchman Nee. I first went to China in 1981. He had already "transferred" to the church triumphant. If I had met him, I would have said, "Thanks. Thanks for helping us in our faith. Now, my Brother Nee, I want to share with you some of the words and blessings of God that you may have missed."

Introduction:
The Journey East

In the early 1960s, Americans grew more accustomed to thinking of China as "inscrutable." The war years of the 1940s and the Cold War years of the 50s made us sympathize with the Chinese people as heroic and oppressed. In 1960, John F. Kennedy and Richard Nixon debated the value of defending two small islands both claimed by the governments of Beijing and of Taipei, Taiwan. There was also the 1930s film image of Charlie Chan on TV. Chan was a Hawaiian Chinese police detective. According to the script, he solved crimes by using the proverbial wisdom of the East and meditating carefully on the evidence. As Charlie Chan said, "Mind like umbrella; work best when open."

Americans had Eisenhower, Proverbs, and Perry Mason. China had Chiang Kai-shek, Confucius, and Charlie Chan. China's calligraphy and art were exotic and far more impressive. China was the mysterious orient. We expected to find James Bond at a Shaolin Temple[3] ... not at a Baptist Church in Baton Rouge, Louisiana. It was in 1961, and in that environment, churches and bookstores started selling Watchman Nee's *The Normal Christian Life*.

---

[3] The priests of the Shaolin Temple in Henan Province, China, trained their students in the discipline and acrobatics of Gung Fu martial arts. Today the original Shaolin Temple has become a popular tourist attraction with live performances. Along the main road there are many new centers of Gung Fu. In the town itself, the most visible structure is the tall, new church. Many experts believe that Henan Province has the highest number of Christians in China.

Under the aura of the orient, I bought my first book by Watchman Nee in 1967. Frankly, I was physically and spiritually a babe. Like a babe, I was eager to crawl around and explore every corner of my faith. I wanted to save time and quickstep to spiritual maturity. I had this foolish, adolescent idea that there was someone out there, a seminary teacher, a spiritual guru, or a spiritual man who could bind all of God's vast wisdom into a limited number of volumes. My pastor enthusiastically recommended Nee's *The Normal Christian Life*. The book didn't say anything particularly new to me about doctrine. But it said something more. Doctrine is more than belief. It is a life attitude. A friend suggested that I go "deeper" and read *The Spiritual Man.*

It took a while to get through the three books. I can't say for sure whether or not *The Spiritual Man* helped. It seemed at the time to be a little too mechanical in its approach. Nee was attempting to uncover a means to make the church mature. The effort to discern the spiritual from the natural (that which Nee called *soulical*) can be an admirable effort to renew the church. As Nee well knew, it can also be an excuse to point a finger. To purify is admirable. But is Nee's the only spiritual way? Is it even the right way?

I was learning from others. I went to a Wesleyan-Arminian graduate school. I went to another school where many on the staff were Calvinists. I had friends and teachers who were Charismatics and Pentecostals. By listening to a broad spectrum of Christians, I understood that no single teacher or single school of theology can reveal everything. Some don't cover a wide enough territory. Others are comprehensive, but too brief. No work of systematic theology can tell us everything. God is too big for that.

The years following 1967 were spent reading and studying more publications. By 1976, I had read enough to write the first edition of this book. Twenty-five years later, additional volumes attributed to Nee have been published.

I do not intend to flatter or condemn. I remain suspicious of unsubstantiated accounts of religious folk heroes. I remained convinced that Nee's thoughts have served some as passports to the Kingdom of God. But passports are rarely clean. They are issued in different countries and at different times. They are stamped and sometimes soiled with the earth of Jerusalem as well as Athens, of China as well as America.

This book represents part of my research and analysis. I hope it will answer some of the questions and penetrate some of the secrets surrounding Watchman Nee as a teacher and theologian.

Watchman Nee died on June 1, 1972. He was in a prison camp in Anhwei Province, China. He wasn't tortured to death. He was nearly seventy, had a bad heart, and died from natural causes. By that year, he had become one of the most popular contemporary theologians.* No longer in the position to preach openly, his published messages now number over fifty volumes. They are translations from Chinese. Sometimes the same message appears in different English translations. News of his death in prison during the Cultural Revolution helped popularize his interpretation of the Bible within the global evangelical movement.

Since the publication of *The Normal Christian Life*, many American churches have undergone change by way of three different renewal movements: the prayer group, the charismatic movement, and the Jesus People Movement. To some extent, the writings of Watchman Nee have been influential in all three.

---

* By 1975, *The Normal Christian Life* alone had been published into more than 440,000 copies in the American edition. A. Donald Fredlund, Publications Secretary, Christian Literature Crusade, personal letter, February 24, 1975.

Beginning in the early 1960s, small unstructured prayer groups developed out of a desire on the part of many church members to meet personal needs, to participate and express themselves in the church, to meet other members, and to attain a clear walk with God/Christ. A prayer group usually involved a time of sharing, prayer, and the study of the Bible and/or a Christian book. Many of these groups began studying Nee's books, particularly *The Normal Christian Life, The Release of the Spirit, What Shall This Man Do?* and *The Normal Christian Worker*. A common sentiment among many prayer groups was the view that in some way the work and the power of the Holy Spirit had abated in the church since the apostolic age. Through the study of books like John Sherrill's *They Speak with Other Tongues,* a part of the prayer group renewal was channeled into the charismatic movement.

The charismatic movement, the largest of the renewal movements, has involved members of all Christian faiths, including Roman Catholic and Orthodox churches. Books dealing with the history of the movement give three significant inceptions: the ministry of Pentecostal minister David J. du Plessis in traditional churches and organizations, the work of the Full Gospel Business Men's Fellowship, and the Reverend Dennis Bennett's confession of speaking in tongues before his Episcopal congregation in Van Nuys, California, on April 3, 1960.[1]

The movement's primary characteristic has been a renewed interest in the *charisms* described in the Book of Acts and First Corinthians, chapters 12-14. The individual reception of these gifts is believed by some to occur after an initial outpouring of the Spirit upon the believer at conversion. The second event is called the Baptism in the Holy Spirit. While remaining within the rich theological traditions of Protestantism and Roman Catholicism, Charismatics have drawn their ideas from writers of varying traditions. Apart from theologians within the movement itself, one of the most widely read thinkers is Watchman Nee.

Nee's books have provided many charismatics with a theological basis to call in question or reject many of the ecstatic outbursts that seemed to hinder the church's primary responsibility to preach Christ. Reading his books on theological anthropology, many Pentecostals and charismatic church leaders became convinced that not all tongue speaking nor all prophecy have their origin in the Holy Spirit. Nor does the presence of true *charismata* necessarily indicate a person's moral integrity.

His books on ecclesiology have provided many with a theological bridge between the structured organization of the denomination and the more spontaneous form of Pentecostal worship. Through *Spiritual Authority, What Shall This Man Do?* and his works on the life of the church, many Charismatics were able to find a comfortable balance between diocesan (district) authority and the Pentecostal tendency toward more lay leadership and participation.

One aspect of the charismatic movement was unexpected and contrary to Nee's vision of the future. The charismatic movement was *ecumenical*. The word has its origins in the Latin and Greek languages and means *universal* or *all the inhabitants*. Prior to the charismatic movement, church leaders from different denominations had formed councils to discuss and cooperate together. In China and in many foreign countries, missionaries had cooperated with workers in different denominations. But ecumenism in the charismatic movement came unannounced and unplanned. People from different denominations had a common experience of the Holy Spirited that united them together for fellowship, for prayer, and for ministry. At one church I attended, Catholic nuns were witnessing to those who came forward to receive Christ as their savior in a Mennonite Church. The leader of the evangelistic meeting was Presbyterian. Before that time, only at the Billy Graham Crusades had there been such cooperation in sharing the Gospel of Jesus Christ.

The young had their own evangelistic and charismatic movement. The Jesus People originated from the missionary activities of a number of conservative evangelists.[2] These ministers preached a new message on a "street level" that would appeal to youth's desire for spiritual revelation, a sense of communal love, and a need for personal involvement with a cause. They recognized that the youth of the counter-culture were not to be enamored with what they called "middle-class churchianity"* of the liberal or legalistically fundamental churches.

Although the movement contains conservative and radical factions, certain beliefs are generally held in common. Salvation is not founded on the basis of intellectual assent to church doctrine, nor on church membership, but on a conversion experience and a continuing personal relationship with God through Christ. Christ's "great commission" to the church is largely carried out through street witnessing, bumper stickers, Jesus marches, and "Jesus Is the Rock" concerts, in a manner most appealing to their own peer groups. Most Jesus People blame the institutionalization of worship and the acceptance of false doctrines as the causes of the church's

---

* The term is used to designate all of the characteristics of the denominations that were rejected. The Jesus People are particularly offended with the church's lack of emphasis on Christ as the source of salvation, the importance of conversion and recognition of the church as the eschatological community. Socially, they would also agree with Pierre Berton's assessment in *The Comfortable Pew*:

The worship of conformity and respectability, which distinguishes the religious establishment, turns religion and Christianity into separate entities. Religion, the cult of the establishment, with its denial of Christian radicalism, its alliance with the status quo, and its awesome social power, is, indeed, often the antithesis of Christianity (Philadelphia and New York: J.B. Lippincott Co. 1961, p. 68).

ills. Their solution is to establish a community of believers led by the Holy Spirit. More radical groups, such as the Children of God, accept an imminent premillennial return of Christ requiring drastic methods of evangelism. With the exception of their own newspapers and tracts, the most popular books are Nee's *The Normal Christian Life, The Normal Christian Church Life,* and among the more ascetic, world-abandoning groups, his *Love Not the World.*

Even the charismatic Indonesian Revival of the 1970s had been affected by Nee's teachings. Although only *The Normal Christian Life* has been published in Malay, the state language, evangelical missionaries carried his writings with them. The Reverend Edwin Stube, an Episcopal missionary to Indonesia, established many congregations on the basis of Nee's eldership concept and instruction on the spiritual life:

> ... I got hold of *The Normal New Testament Church Life [sic]* this revolutionized my thinking about the New Testament order in the church. We have been trying to apply all these principles in our fellowship here and in the congregations we founded in the villages. Other books which have helped our understanding of certain aspects of the Christian life have been *Sit, Walk, Stand, Changed into His Likeness,* and most deep of all the commentary, *Song of Songs.* At one point in the life of our community, here we began to receive much new light on God's present purpose in the church particularly in the formation of a people for end-time ministry. Then we got a copy of *The Glorious Church* and were surprised to see that he had been teaching all the exact same things 30 years ago.[3]

An increased interest in biblical and theological sources of faith, a reemphasis on lay participation and leadership, and the experiencing of charismatic authority all contributed to Nee's current notoriety. But the primary reason for his popularity among all renewal groups was his "understanding of spiritual things." As Ellis Larson has shown, the primary emphasis of the church renewal groups was the dynamics of the Spirit.[4] These dynamics have as their focal point the concept of a spiritual reality, which many have discovered through the works of Watchman Nee.

Within the membership and variety of all these groups was a desire for personal experience or communion with God. The writings of contemporary theologians proved inadequate, too complicated, or spurious. The works of Paul Tillich, Karl Barth and Søren Kierkegaard appealed to individuals far more theoretical or intellectual than the general populace of the church. On the other hand, Nee's books were more meaningful to the faith seekers. They were directly personal and spoke of knowing as something spiritual and without a sophisticated theological language. And yet *The Spiritual Man, The Latent Power of the Soul, Christ: The Sum of All Spiritual Things,* and others attributed to the Bible sublime secrets to be recovered by men with spiritual knowledge—spiritual men.

Believers expect the meaning and message of the Bible to be more profound than any other classical work of literature. This view is inherent in Nee's conception of the Bible, which he asserted to be in accord with all true knowledge of God:

> If a person is not regenerated, then no matter how clever and scholarly he may be, to him this book is a mystery. But a regenerated man whose cultural background may be quite primitive possesses greater understanding of the Bible than does an unregenerated college professor. And the explanation? One of them has a regenerated spirit, while the other has not. The Scriptures cannot be mastered through cleverness, research, or natural talent. The Word of God is spirit, therefore it can only be known to whoever possesses a regenerated spirit. Since the root and the nature of the Bible are spiritual, how can anyone who lacks a

regenerated spirit begin to understand it? It is a closed book to him.[5]

While this idea is one of the finer points of his writings, it is also the most vulnerable to criticism for establishing a form of Gnosticism and fostering spiritual pride.

Since that time, there have been setbacks in these renewal movements. The Jesus People lost credibility when Jesus did not return in the 1980s, as their favorite end-times teacher had predicted. Many charismatic pastors and leaders were involved with public scandals related to money and sex. Some sought to renew the government with Christian leaders and uncompromising commitment to traditional values. Other Americans regarded them as ridiculous and out of fashion. Ground was lost and tithes needlessly consumed when Christians sought vindication in the secular courts. Lawyers and mammon replaced God as the final arbiter of orthodoxy. Yet, sales of some of Watchman Nee's books continued to soar.

The 1990s brought reports of revival experiences in Toronto, Canada, Brownsville, Texas, and Pensacola, Florida. Laughing, crying, dancing, and barking like a dog are ether with an outpouring of praise and worship. The Christian community is divided on its meaning. Both sides recommend Watchman Nee as vindication.

Because Nee is a popular pathfinder in the modern church's quest for lasting spiritual renewal, his qualifications and his choice of methods need to be questioned. What training and life experiences prepared him to lead others on the way to spiritual maturity? Is the Bible, inspired by the Holy Spirit, the sole compass of his faith? Or has some less accurate device detoured him away from the Christian "walk in newness of life" (Romans 6:4)? Are his ideas pragmatic? In other words, do they really do what he says they will do?

The aim of this book is to answer these, and to provide a thorough survey and analysis of his life and thought. The first chapter deals with his life and ministry. Besides providing an overview of Nee's life and that of the "Little Flock,"* a reconstruction of the theological roots of Nee's beliefs according to his Christian education will be given. Sources for this biography include Nee's own testimony, historical sources, and secondary biographies. The chapter will conclude with a history of the Little Flock under the influence of Nee's co-worker and chief exponent, Witness Lee.

Chapter two is a brief description of Nee's voluminous works and presents a historical, textual, and stylistic appraisal upon which to evaluate the content of Nee's theology. The next three chapters serve as the core of this thesis and analyze Nee's theology in three areas: the Word of God, anthropology, and ecclesiology. This book ends with a summary of the evidence and a conclusion.

---

* The churches founded by Nee and his co-workers are hesitant to label their movement as a whole. Outsiders have given them this term from *The Little Flock Hymnal*, which they published and used in their services.

Introduction Endnotes

1. Michael Harper, *As at the Beginning: The Twentieth Century Pentecostal Revival* (Plainfield, NJ.: Logos International, 1965), pp, 51-79; Walter J. Hollenweger, *The Pentecostals: The Charismatic Movement in the Churches* (Minneapolis: Augsburg Publishing House, 1972), pp. 3-17; John Thomas Nichol, *The Pentecostals* (Plainfield, NJ.: Logos International, 1966), pp. 240-45; and John L. Sherrill, *They Speak with Other Tongues*, Spire ed. (Westwood NJ.: Fleming H. Revell Co., 1965), pp. 51-67.

2. For a history of the movement: Ronald M. Enroth, Edward E. Ericson, Jr., and C. Breckinridge Peters, *The Jesus People: Old Time Religion in the Age of Aquarius* (Grand Rapids: Wm. B. Eerdmans Publishing Co., 1972), pp. 21-157.

3. Rev. Edwin Stube to Dana Roberts, Feb. 16, 1975, personal letter.

4. Ellis Leif Larson, "Where Preachers Dare! (An Empirical Evaluation of the Church Renewal Phenomena in the 1960's)" (Ann Arbor, Mich.: University Microfilms, 73-10, 251, 1972).

5. Watchman Nee, *Ye Search the Scriptures* (New York: Christian Fellowship Publishers, Inc., 1974), p. 15.

CHAPTER ONE

Watchman Nee and the Work of the Little Flock

In the century before 1949, the nation of China underwent two cultural revolutions. The first, brought about by European commercial and imperial interests, resulted in a cultural shift from Oriental custom to Occidental tradition in matters of government, technology, and social structure. The second, concurrent in time and location with the first, established Christianity as a numerically significant religion in China. In essence, the historical and cultural setting of Watchman Nee's career and teachings are reflective of the conflict and harmony existing in the Oriental, Occidental, and Christian cultures.*

---

* The brief biography that follows is largely taken from the only significant biographies of Watchman Nee in English. The first, *Against the Tide* (Fort Washington, Pa.: Christian Literature Crusade, 1973), was written by medical missionary Angus Kinnear. His book presents us Watchman Nee as a sympathetic character who desired above all to know more about Christ. In 1991, Witness Lee published a far different biography. Typical of the preference for hyperbole, he entitled the book *Watchman Nee: A Seer of the Divine Revelation in the Present Age* (Anaheim, CA: Living Stream Ministry, 1991). Kinnear shows Nee as humble servant wanting more of Christ's victory in his life. Lee's Nee is a suffering seer seeking vindication.

Parents and Native Residence

On October 19, 1899, Nee Wen-Hsiu of Foochow, a maritime customs officer serving in Swatow, married Lin Ho-P'ing, the adopted daughter of a wealthy businessman. Although the service was performed in a Christian (Anglican) church in Nan-t'ai, the marriage had been arranged according to Oriental custom, and the conjugal celebrants had not met before the day of their wedding.

Wen-Hsiu's father, Nee U-Cheng, was a congregational minister affiliated with the American Board of Missions, headquartered in the district capitol of Foochow.* As a result, of the Treaty of Nanking (1842) that ended the Opium War, Foochow had become one of the first successful Protestant missionary centers in China. Under the terms of the treaty, Great Britain and China both agreed to protect trading and missionary posts in the five ports of Canton, Amoy, Shanghai, Ningpo, and Foochow. Missions were quickly established in Foochow, first by the Boston-based American Board, followed shortly by the Anglicans and the Episcopal Methodists. But the religious victories won in the Nan-king Treaty became a hindrance to effective evangelism. Missionaries came to rely too heavily on the military arm of the British Consulate,† and the local population began associating Christianity with "imperialism." This particularly affected the Anglican missions, whom the people associated with the British opium trade.§

Nevertheless, in 1853, Nga U-Cheng, Watchman Nee's grandfather, was won over to the Christian message. He then began attending the American Board's school established

---

* Located twenty-five miles upstream from the mouth of the River Minchiang, Foochow is a commercial city known for its tea and orange trade. In 1920, its population exceeded 624,000.[1]
† Prime Minister Lord Salisbury at the bicentennial meeting of the Society for the Propagation of the Gospel (1900) said, "But now if a Boniface or a Columba [names of churches] is exposed to these martyrdoms, the result is an appeal to the consul and the mission of a gunboat ... I must not

2

outside of Foochow. Records of the Foochow mission show a prescribed number of books in the school's required curriculum. Included among these was John L. Nevius's three-volume theology, *Compendium of Theology*. As a missionary to China himself, Nevius (1829-93) offered the Chinese an explanation for the apparent diversity of ethics among self-professed (Western) Christians. Sanctification, he argued, involved "a psychological battle between soul and spirit."[5] Therefore, new Christians should understand that not all believers live according to the spirit. By 1857, U-Cheng had learned his lesson well enough to become a baptized member. Recognized by his Occidental superiors as a natural preacher, he became the second ordained Chinese minister of the congregational mission in Fukien Province on June 4, 1876.[6]

In 1877-1878, China underwent a severe drought and famine. Hudson Taylor, the founder of the China Inland Mission, saw this as an opportunity for foreign Christians to truly love their neighbors as themselves. He also saw it as a way of showing that faith does indeed lead to good works of charity. The poor clearly saw this. The church grew because it fed and cared for the poor and even took care of abandoned baby girls. The rice and care were free. The food, as well as love, was given without condition of conversion.

Many churches were established among the poorest of the people. Many Chinese workers received financial assistance from the foreign missions. A harmless, charitable

---

conceal from you that at the Foreign Office, the missionaries are not popular."[2]

§ "I weep over the melancholy fact, but I cannot wonder at it whoever else may do so: for our Chinese missionaries have all along been counteracted by the influence of the opium trade."[3] Chinese anti-Christian literature assumed that native converts had been given a thought-controlling pill.[4]

act. Yet, the imperial government spread the rumor that these workers had abandoned the faith of their ancestors for money or for rice. Having a large family, U-cheng was given a salary of eleven dollars a month, a substantial sum of money by nineteenth-century Chinese standards. One year later, his fourth son, Wen-Hsiu, was born.

A few days after his father's death (1890), Wen-Hsiu took the three-day-long Confucian competitive examinations. These exams were tests of classical skills in literature, which the imperial government used to determine who could best serve in civil positions as representatives of Chinese tradition. Wen-Hsiu was awarded the second-degree level, ensuring him a job in the government for the rest of his life. His job would provide enough money to have a family and leave behind a life of poverty.

The life of Ho-P'ing, his wife and Watchman Nee's mother, had been far more difficult. A strong influence on her son's personal and spiritual development, her life was expressive of the cross-cultural shift so characteristic of the period of China's greatest church growth. Born into a large non-Christian family during the famine of 1880, she was sold by her father to a family that was better off.* She was again sold to a merchant named Lin of Nan-ta'i. Although the merchant loved children, he adhered to the aesthetic tradition of foot binding.†

The same year as Ho-P'ing's adoption, Mr. Lin became seriously ill with a mysterious disease that was undiagnosable and untreatable by both Chinese and Western doctors. Upon

---

* Some of Ho-P'ing's peers fared much worse. Infanticide was a common practice. (See footnote 8.)
† In this procedure, each foot was bound tightly so that the yet unossified heel and tarsus were forced together. Each day the binding was tightened further in a manner that ensured continuous pain until she reached physical maturity. The idea was to produce "lily feet" that could fit into a teacup.

the recommendation of one of Lin's business associates, they sought out the aid of a Methodist pastor who believed in healing. A dramatic recovery followed. Just as dramatic was the change in the Lin household. The family idols were discarded. Mr. Lin and his wife were baptized into the Methodist church. Ho-P'ing's painful foot binding ended, and she, according to her own testimony, rejoiced in the hymns and Bible stories taught her.

Like most Christians, her new life was not always harmonious with her consecration. While attending the Chinese Western Girls School in Shanghai in preparation for an American medical school education, Ho-P'ing became involved in worldly interests and pleasures. In her autobiography, *An Object of Grace and Love*, she writes, "I learned there much of the pride of life and some of the sins of the flesh."[7] Once moved by the faith of a young visiting missionary, Miss Dora Yu, she was still unwilling to give up her interests. Her weakness for worldly things would again reveal itself years after her marriage.

Completing her English studies in Shanghai, her plans to travel to America met with disappointment. Her mother opposed her trip and permanently delayed it by arranging a marriage for her adopted daughter with the son of the late Pastor Nga (Nee in Fukien dialect). She was bound by custom, for no Fukien girl had ever broken a marriage arrangement.

Birth and Early Education

Four years after her marriage, Nee Ho-P'ing was in distress with the expectancy of her third child. Her first two both had been girls, a personal disgrace to her responsibilities as a bearer of the male heir. Her mother-in-law feared she would be like the wife of her eldest son, who bore six children—all females. In her anguish, Ho-P'ing promised that if the Lord gave her a boy, she would return him back for His service.

5

On November 4, 1903, in Swatow, a male child, Nee Shu-Tsu, was born. His name means "he who proclaims his ancestors' merits." Years later, after the boy's mission in life became more evident, she proposed a new name, To-Sheng, "the sound of a gong." The name would remind both mother and son that he would be a "bell ringer" (or Watchman) who would raise the people of God for service.

Shortly thereafter, the Nee family returned to their ancestral home of Foochow. There Watchman began his education in both classical and Christian studies. A tutor appointed by the elder Nee instructed him in calligraphy, the ethical maxims contained in the traditional Four Books and Five Classics, and the Chinese musical system called The Melodies. In hand with this Oriental instruction, his mother taught him Christian hymns and Bible lessons. In all, Nee showed intellectual promise.

But by 1912, it became apparent that a classical tradition was no longer as important as it once had been in attaining vocational success. The two hundred sixty-eight-year, archaic Manchu Dynasty had been overthrown, and Sun Yat-Sen's *Kuomintang* appeared to be gaining the support of a majority of the people. With its slogans of "Love One's Country" and "Nationalism, Democracy and Livelihood," the movement popularized the benefits of Western culture, including its educational values. The long, plaited queues were cut off, and Western educational institutions benefited with increased enrollment.

In the Nee household, Sun Yat-Sen became the family hero. As an advocate of women's rights, Sun was particularly appealing to Nee's mother. Through her lectures and correspondence, Ho-P'ing founded the local Women's Patriotic Society. Her husband was less enthusiastic; he desired that Watchman should receive a Western-Christian education. He sent Nee to three schools: The Church

Missionary Society's vernacular school, St. Mark's High School (English) and, finally, Trinity College.

Trinity College, Foochow, had been founded by W.S. Packenham-Walsh, a former student of the Anglican Trinity College in Dublin, Ireland. Commissioned by the Church Missionary Society, he went to Fukien with the sincere hope of preaching Christ and ridding the community there of such habits as foot binding, infanticide,* and the custom of some widows of hanging themselves publicly to be reunited with their departed husbands. Nevertheless, he was a product of the Victorian Age and never permitted his English dignity to be relaxed so that all men might hear his message. Wherever he went, he always wanted a tablecloth on his eating table as a mark of civilization. Once when he was crossing a river, he permitted some people to ride in the boat with him. But when one of his fellow passengers boarded a flock of goats, he later wrote, "This I felt was exceedingly the limits even of Christian toleration, so I had them all turned out ..."[10]

His missionary efforts met with greater success when he offered the Chinese something they desired—a quality education. By 1905, he had purchased the property of the former Russian Consulate on the Black Stone Hill in Foochow and established a junior college there. He named it in honor of his alma mater and staffed it with Dublin professors. The school instructed and preached the gospel by interpreting Chinese classics in the light of the Bible. The Word was also ministered through Anglican matins given in Chinese.

Nee found the school's paramilitary form of discipline with its "Western" form of worship not to his liking. In a

---

* Near the school, a baby tower had been constructed to provide a burial place for the children of the poor. Like the trash and dung heaps of the Roman Empire,[8] it became the place to discard unwanted children .[9] Generally, they were baby girls. Even today nearly all Chinese children given up for adoption or abortion are girls.

testimony given some fifteen years after leaving college, Nee reflected on his attitude toward Christianity and preaching at that time:

> Formerly I had despised preachers and preaching because in those days most preachers were the employees of European or American missionaries, having to be servile to them, and earning merely eight or nine dollars each month. I had never imagined for a moment that I would become a preacher, a profession that I regarded as trifling and base.[11]

While some students were converted by the Church of England propers given in the chapel services, Nee clearly sided with many of the senior students who demonstrated a proclivity to antireligious sentiments.

And there was plenty of antireligious feeling at the time. Before the century even began, many Chinese saw Western missions as a form of colonialism. There was justification for this. European governments, especially Germany, used antimissionary riots as an excuse to control more territory. The churches were controlled by the foreigners. The Chinese ruling elite resented their work. They believed that authority comes from assimilating the truths of Confucius and becoming perfect men. The missions established schools that taught both men and women math, science, and the Bible ... not the Chinese classics. The criticism continued for so many years that many Western-educated Christians who had benefited the most from the denominational missions were the most insistent that the foreign missions should neither teach nor lead local churches. Watchman Nee was just one of them. Others saw the problem in a different light. It was not a matter surrender power. Church planters in China as well as America are reluctant to delegate leadership in the churches the founded, even after the foundation of Christ had been firmly laid.[12]

His dissatisfaction with Christianity affirmed itself in his academic activities. An excellent student in all subjects except the Bible, Nee preferred to read cheap novels that were smuggled into the school rather than to labor over the Scripture. Consequently, to save face with his Christian parents, he resorted to cheating in order to pass his Bible exams.

Conversion

Concurrent with this time, Nee's mother had received a place of honor for her political activities. Society ladies began coming to her house and introducing her to the pursuits of the elite: playing cards and mah-jong. Thereafter, her interests turned away from religion and politics to social pleasure.

Her lapse of faith became evident to Watchman when in January of 1920 she wrongly accused him of breaking a valuable ornament. Though he refused to confess, she gave him a thrashing. Later she discovered his innocence in the matter, but she was without remorse, and according to tradition did not admit her error to her son out of pride in her position in the family.*

A month later Miss Dora Yu, the woman evangelist who had impressed Ho-P'ing earlier, began revival meetings in the Methodist Tien-An Chapel.[13] In respect for their former association, Ho-P'ing attended the first services. Convicted by the Holy Spirit, she soon told her gambling friends, "I am a Christian, Miss Yu has come a long distance to preach here … I shall not play tomorrow!"[14] She later became a well-known Methodist preacher, whose speaking tours included her native China and Malaya.

Under the strong conviction of her sins, she tearfully went to Watchman to seek forgiveness. Before her husband

---

* In the Confucian tradition, the instruction of filial piety requires that a parent should never submit to her children.

9

and her children, she threw her arms around him and cried, "For the Lord Jesus' sake, I confess to beating you unjustly and in anger."[15] He at first seemed little moved by her confession, but that same night, he also became a convert to Christ:

> On the evening of 29th April, 1920, I was alone in my room, struggling to decide whether or not to believe in the Lord. At first, I was reluctant, but as I tried to pray, I saw the magnitude of my sins and the reality and efficacy of Jesus as the Savior. As I visualized the Lord's hands stretched out on the cross, they seemed to be welcoming me, and the Lord was saying, "I am waiting here to receive you." Realizing the effectiveness of Christ's blood in cleansing my sins and being overwhelmed by such love, I accepted him there. Previously I had laughed at people who had accepted Jesus, but that evening the experience became real for me and I wept and confessed my sins, seeking the Lord's forgiveness. As I made my first prayer, I knew joy and peace such as I had never known before. Light seemed to flood the room and I said to the Lord, "Oh Lord, you have indeed been gracious to me."[16]

The next day he attended one of Miss Yu's meetings and openly proclaimed his salvation by going forward.

Stimulated perhaps by his mother's example, Nee believed that "Christian repentance includes the confession of past faults,"[17] in addition to a change of conduct. He no longer cheated in his Bible tests, and he openly confessed to the school principal that he had written the answers to tests on his palms. The normal procedure for this type of rule infraction was expulsion. Because of his honesty, however, the principal declined to dismiss him. Except for a one-year absence in which he attended Miss Yu's Bible school in Shanghai, Nee continued his studies at Trinity, vigorously witnessing to his friends and fellow students.

Theological Education

Discarding much of his theological training at Trinity, a majority of Nee's teachings and exegetical methods are traceable to instruction received apart from his formal schooling. Two Bible schools, extensive theological reading, and a methodical study of the Bible subsequent to his college education are responsible for much of the depth of his teaching.

During the 1920-21 school period, he stayed at Miss Yu's Bible school in Shanghai. From her he learned to let the Holy Spirit speak to his own heart through God's Word. Memorizing Scripture texts was important, but one had to permit the Scripture to be an instrument of God's will through revelation. Miss Yu also taught him to trust in the Lord for his needs and not to be concerned with worldly pursuits. This instruction proved to be a difficult message for him and was one of the reasons that led him to seek a "second blessing." In his own testimony, he admitted to being a "fleshly or carnal believer"[15] and to the irreconcilability of his actions and the school's discipline:

> Before very long she politely expelled me from the institute with the explanation that it was inconvenient for me to stay any longer. Because of my gourmet appetite, dilettante dress and tardy arising in the mornings Sister Yu thought fit to send me home. My desire to serve the Lord had been dealt a serious blow. Although I thought my life had been transformed, in fact there remained many more things to be changed.[19]

Even though Nee had seen some fruit, he was not satisfied with his Christian growth:

---

* This is the term used by Nee for those Christians who are dominated by some natural necessity of the human body (nourishment, reproduction, and defense).[18]

Free from Worldliness?

Besides giving up fine clothes, Nee's long-time friend and coworker Witness Lee says that Nee "would not observe any festival or celebrate a birthday because to his enlightened understanding these things were worldly." Nee also thought that going to the movies was sinful. The author goes on to say, "Because he dealt with worldliness in such a strict fashion, he was continually kept in the presence of God."[22]

That's a remarkable, yet true statement. How did Lee know that Watchman Nee was continually kept in the presence of God? Nee, like *every* Christian, is kept in the presence of God. It has nothing to do with tailor-made clothes or with observing holidays or not observing them. Our robes of righteousness are not enough (Isaiah 54:6). Assurance comes when we follow two commandments: Have faith in the Lord Jesus Christ and love the brothers. We are then clothed in Christ and His righteous love (Galatians 3:27, Col. 3:12-14; 1 John 3:18-24. There's nothing here to suggest avoiding birthday parties.

Witness Lee may be forgiven for exercising hyperbole and hagiography, the ancient tradition of Saint-making. Yet, Lee cannot exaggerate Christ's righteousness that enables a crucified thief as well as the oldest of saints to stand in the presence of God.

Though some people had been saved, I was not satisfied, since many in the school and in the town were unaffected, and I felt the need to be filled with the Holy Spirit and to receive power from above.[20]

At Dora Yu's suggestion, he went to Miss M.E. Barber, a British missionary. She instructed him in the Keswick concept of the victorious life through the filling of the Holy Spirit.

I returned to school to seek the filling of the Holy Spirit and the love of Christ, but I found that I still could not say with conviction the words of the Psalm [Ps. 73:25]. At last, on February 13th, 1922, I was willing to lay aside this relationship [with Chang Pin-huei (Charity), his future wife, who at this time was not a Christian] and then I knew an experience of great elation. On the day I was converted, I shook off the burden of my sins, but on this later occasion, my heart was emptied of everything that would separate me from God. From then on people began to be saved. On that day I changed my fine clothes for a simple garment, went into the kitchen, made some paste, and with a bundle of gospel posters on my arm, went out into the street to post them on the walls and to distribute gospel tracts. In those days in Foochow, Fukien Province, this was a pioneer act. From the second term of 1922, I prayed daily for those school friends whose names were in my notebook, and many of them were saved.[21]

These quotes indicate that clothes served as one measure of Nee's sense of holiness and his avoidance of worldly pursuits. And yet, Angus Kinnear's biography shows a studio photograph of Nee wearing a fine business suit. It is difficult to say when the picture was taken. Yet, Nee is clearly older than he was in the image taken on his wedding day in 1934. Is this an inconsistency? A change of heart?

During the first seven years following his "baptism in the Holy Spirit," Nee's ministry rapidly expanded. Because of the revival at Trinity College, Nee received the assistance of a number of co-workers in his ministry to the school and the surrounding towns and provinces. In 1923 he began the publication of religious materials, including the magazine *The Present Testimony*, and went on numerous speaking tours, practices that continued to be a part of his ministry until his arrest during Mao Tse-tung's "Cultural Revolution." The relative success of the work caused Nee to conclude that his movement had a relatively clear "understanding of the gospel of grace."[23] But he desired to further clarify in his own mind the distinction between grace and law; the kingdom of heaven and eternal life; grace and reward; and salvation and victory.[24] At the suggestion of Dora Yu, Nee sought the instruction of a teacher more mature than himself in the ways of the Lord, Miss Margaret E. Barber.

Like Nee, Miss Barber had become disenchanted with Anglican doctrine and polity. In 1909 while on furlough from her missionary post at the Nan-t'ai girls' middle school, she began to seriously question the church's position on infant baptism. To the dismay of her bishop, she began attending the services at the independent Surrey Chapel, Norwich. Under the teaching of Rev. David M. Panton, she adjudged baptism to be actually a baptism into the Lord's death. In this death, they believed that the believer separated himself from the "world" and its perdition.[25] Just as Christ's death concluded with the resurrection unto life, so also the believer received resurrection into the church with newness of life.*

In 1920 after severing her ties with the Anglican Church Missionary Society, she returned to China as an independent missionary under the sponsorship of Surrey Chapel. In short time she was joined by her friend Miss L.S. Ballord and an independent Chinese woman preacher, Li Ai-ming. Feeling that God was calling them to train natives for church leadership, they rented a twenty-room building to serve as a school. In a manner testifying to this witness, Watchman Nee and many who had become Christians through his and Miss Yu's ministry† attended her classes and personal instruction on the spiritual life.

---

* "The Fourfold Work of the Cross" in chapter 4.
† One student, Leland Wang, founded the China Overseas Missionary Union in Indonesia and continues to be active in a Hong Kong church.[26]

Good Reading for Devoted Readers

In *Watchman Nee: A Seer of the Divine Revelation in the Present Age*, the author says that Nee was a devoted reader of the Bible and spiritual books. My late Aunt Betty used to say, "That's a pious answer if ever I heard one." Yet, the Apostle Paul knew well the ideas of Epicureans and Stoics (Acts 17:16-33). In Titus 1:12-13, he quotes and acknowledges that Epimendes was a prophet among the Cretans. Is Paul or anyone else less spiritual if we read widely? We're all fully human. Even "spiritual" writers can make mistakes. Some men must work the fields all the day. Others can read the Bible and the classics of piety all day. Both are daily tempted to use the razor-sharp, two-edged sword of the Lord into cutting words of carnal malpractice.[28]

No single person is more responsible for the development of Nee's theology than Miss Barber is. While he later rejected her teaching ministry to men as inappropriate to the woman's responsibility in the church, he repeatedly acknowledged her influence as a "light" in his own life.[27] Despite this difference of opinion, he continued to seek her advice and counsel until shortly before her death in May 1930. As evidence of her own affection for him, Miss Barber designated in her will that he receive her most prized possession, her Bible.

A devoted reader, Nee took advantage of Miss Barber's library. There he availed himself of much of the holiness literature influential in Great Britain because of the Keswick Movement and the Welsh Revival.[27] Their significance in his own studies is corroborated by his frequent references to such holiness writers as Andrew Murray, Evan Roberts, T. Austin Sparks, and Jessie Penn-Lewis. Some of these books even provided the essential outline of thought to his own books. Mrs. Jessie Penn-Lewis (1861-1927), the Welsh teacher and evangelist, set the tone for the spiritual and anthropological emphasis of Nee's writings.*

A feature of all of Mrs. Penn-Lewis' literature is the theme of "spiritual warfare" among the parts of man's nature. In her books on the cross, the "flesh" must be crucified so that the human spirit, the "god-consciousness" of man, is active.[30] The "I" of the old creation must be yielded to the cross, so that man, no longer loving his "soul"—the "self-consciousness"— can walk "not after the flesh, but after the spirit."[31] Once the human spirit has been released from the bondage of the soul, it may be open to the Holy Spirit's leading.

The high regard that both Watchman Nee and M.E. Barber shared for this Welsh lady is brought to light in this narrative taken from Angus Kinnear's biography:

> He asked Miss Barber if she could not lend him something to read on the subject of the cross. Yes, she said, she had two books, but she would not give them to him at present; she would rather wait until he was mature enough to read them. "I could not understand the reason

---

* Raised in a Calvinistic Methodist home in Wales, Jessie Penn-Lewis suffered from a chronic, debilitating lung ailment throughout her life. After her marriage to an accountant, she began attending services at Holy Trinity Church in Richmond, Surrey. The pastor, the Reverend Evan H. Hopkins, a leading theologian of the early Keswick Conventions, preached victory over sins through the cross of Christ, full surrender to Him, and an imbuement with power for service subsequent to conversion. In complete accord with this Keswick theology, she later became a lecturer and author on the "abundant life." When the Welsh Revival started in 1902, she had wholly supported it as "the rushing mighty breath upon the land." But when religious enthusiasm turned into uncontrolled ecstasy, Mrs. Penn-Lewis, together with Evan Roberts, became one of its most well known critics. After the revival, she considered it her particular ministry to set up "consultative conferences" to instruct believers about the spiritual warfare and the work of Satan in counterfeiting spiritual reality. Her battle plans for this psychic war and anthropological struggle dominated the three booklets she wrote during this period (*War on the Saints, The Spiritual Warfare and Soul and Spirit*). Her last book's emphasis on dividing of soul and spirit according to Heb. 4:12 reinforced the formulation of Nee's theology.

for this," he says, "and I wanted those two books very much, so I obtained them by guile. I inquired from her the titles and author without her realizing what I was doing, and I wrote off to Mrs. Penn-Lewis, who sent them to me as a gift and wrote me a nice letter as well! One was *The Word of the Cross* and the other *The Cross and Its Message*. Well, I read them most carefully, but though I received help of a kind, to my disappointment they didn't settle my biggest question. That, I find, is not God's way, to give us quick answers."[32]

Both Barber and Nee subscribed to her magazine, *The Overcomer*,* which permitted them to become familiar with Andrew Murray, F.B. Meyer, Madame Guyon, and George Müller.

With some reservation, Miss Barber lent him her Plymouth Brethren collection of expository writings by C.A. Coates and J. Nelson Darby. Much pleased by their sense of revelation, he wrote to Mr. George Ware, a London publisher, and received copies of books by C.H. Mackintosh (*Notes on the Pentateuch*), William Kelly, Charles Stanley, and George Cutting, whose booklet "Safety, Certainty, and Enjoyment" was a favorite of Nee. In 1945, in a series of messages, Nee summarized the influence of the Brethren upon his thought and that of the churches he founded:

> They showed us how the blood of the Lord satisfies the righteousness of God; the assurance of salvation; how the weakest believer may be accepted in Christ, just as Christ was accepted; how to believe in the Word of God as the foundation of salvation. Since church history began, there never was a period when the gospel was clearer

---

* The magazine was founded in 1909 and continues to be published by the Overcomer Literature Trust. The single emphasis on teaching faith is evident in the issues printed during World War II. The only reference to the war was an obituary about one of the magazine's secretaries who was killed during an air raid.

than in that time. Not only so, it was also they who showed us that the church cannot gain the entire world, that the church has a heavenly calling, and that the church has no worldly hope. It was they who also opened up prophecies for the first time, causing us to see that the return of the Lord is the hope of the church. It was they who opened the Book of Revelation and the Book of Daniel and showed us the kingdom, the tribulation, the rapture, and the bride. Without them, we would have known today a very small percentage of future things. It was also they who showed us what the law of sin is, what it is to be set free, what it is to be crucified with Christ, what it is to be raised with Christ, how to be identified with the Lord through faith, and how to be transformed daily by looking unto Him. It was they who showed us the sin of denominations, the unity of the Body of Christ, and the unity of the Holy Spirit. It was they who showed us the difference between Judaism and the Church. In the Roman Catholic Church and the Protestant churches, this difference could not be readily seen, but they made us see it anew. It was also they who showed us the sin of the mediatorial class, how all the children of God are priests, and how all can serve God. It was they who recovered for us the principle of meetings in I Corinthians 14, showing us that prophesying is not based upon ordination, but upon the gift of the Holy Spirit. If we were to enumerate one by one what they recovered, we may as well say that in today's pure Protestant churches there is not one truth that they had recovered or recovered more.[33]

As his work expanded, Nee endeavored to keep a soundly scriptural basis for his theology and to preserve himself within the historic "witness of the Spirit" within the church. In studying the Bible, he supplemented his own insights with that of C.I. Scofield, Robert Young, Samuel P. Tregelles, F.W. Grant, Henry Alford, B.F. Westcott, and J.B. Lightfoot.

Beyond Brethren and Keswick materials, Nee read and studied the lives of such diverse church figures as Hudson

Taylor, John Bunyon, A.B. Simpson, Sadhu Sundar Singh, Dwight L. Moody, Charles G. Finney, C.H. Spurgeon, John Wesley, Jonathan Edwards, David Brainerd, Martin Luther, John Knox, George Whitefield, and Cardinal John Henry Newman.

Denominations, Suffering and Persecution

In 1922, Watchman Nee was excommunicated because of his strong opposition to anything connected with denominations. Excommunication can mean to shun someone ... not talk to them because of the seriousness of their sinful life. The other meaning is withholding the church's Holy Communion from them. The latter seems to be the case here. The irony is that Nee was excommunicated for refusing to share in Holy Communion with people who remained in denominations. From that year on, denominational churches criticized Nee. He criticized the denominations for criticizing him.

Development of the Little Flock

Nee's legacy to the contemporary church is not limited to his voluminous writings. While there has been a large number of Christian writers in the two millennia of the church, Nee shares with a much smaller group the distinction of being a founder of a sect within Christendom. Dividing himself from other denominations quite early in the Christian life, his church began in a much more auspicious way than the Methodist or Lutheran Church.

One of Miss Yu's students, Leland Wang (Wang Tsai), had a room large enough to serve as a place for believers and students to come together for prayer and Bible study. In 1922 Wang, his wife, Watchman, and his mother began to meet there. As is the custom of such informal meetings, each shared a testimony of what God was doing in his or her life and prayed for the particular needs of the group or for the needs of others. While none of them was official clergy, they felt the real need to "show the Lord's death"[34] by sharing the Lord's Supper. Through this lay worship, they had a real sense of "joy and release" that communicated itself to others, and in a few weeks, others joined them.

Like Charles Wesley's "Holy Club" at Oxford, they felt a real responsibility to the community and actively campaigned for the Lord through religious processions and evangelistic rallies. They adopted the custom of wearing "gospel shirts"— long white cotton sheets which carried short Bible verses in large Chinese characters: "Repent and believe the gospel;" "God so loved the world." Beating drums and singing hymns as they went, they would gather large crowds into rented halls to hear their message or that of Miss Ruth Lee, a converted atheist.

For three years this type of ministry continued. But problems arose between Leland Wang, the real head of the group, and Watchman Nee. Despite the efforts of Miss Barber to heal the relationship, Nee was reluctant to submit to the decisions of Wang that he considered unscriptural.

Ironically, the disagreement was over the unity of the church. Nee contended that their ministry should not just emotionally stir up the people, but they should work to form new churches that would minister continually a life-giving message. In his characteristic style, he described how he discovered his error through an inner, anthropological revelation:

> I had to admit that even when I was right by human standards, the inner life pronounced me wrong . . . .. From that day I began to see more and more clearly that in relation to any course of action, even if others pronounced it right, and I myself considered it right, and every aspect of the case indicated that it was right, I must still be very sensitive to the reactions of the life of Christ within me. As we advance in the approved course, does the inner life

grow stronger or weaker? Does the inner "anointing" confirm the rightness of the course, or does an absence of the "anointing" indicate that the divine approval is withheld? God's way for us is not known by external indications but by internal registrations. It is peace and joy in the spirit that indicate the Christian's path.[35]

In 1925 on the suggestion of Wang, Nee went with his mother to Sitiawan, Malaya, for a speaking tour. Their meetings there met with some success, despite the fact that most of the natives were more interested in tapping rubber trees than in "touching spiritual reality."[36] It did give him time to pray for direction, and upon his return to China, he formally broke from the Foochow group and established his headquarters in the neighborhood of Pagoda.

During his ministry at Pagoda, Nee made a number of trips to the areas of Amoy, Julongsu, Changchow, and Tungan. Speaking to large groups within and outside of traditional churches, Nee would take down the names of those who responded to his messages and send them copies of his *Revival Magazine.*

At one visit to the Talmadge College and Seminary of the American Presbyterian Mission, Nee met his old associate Ruth Lee. She was working with the Spiritual Light Publishing Society, and persuaded him to work there, also. For a few months, he worked faithfully for them in Nanking, but his own attitude towards Western missions would reaffirm itself as a result of a strain in Christian-pagan relations.

Like a recurring nightmare, anti-missionary riots broke out in Foochow and Shanghai, and the death of Sun Yat-sen made the fate of international groups uncertain. While some semblance of civil order was restored under the Commander-in-Chief of the Army, Chiang Kai-shek, Nee was determined to form a new church totally non-Western and based upon the concept of one church for one locality.

Not long after, however, serious illness would temporarily postpone his preaching plans, giving him an opportunity to prepare his messages. In Shanghai, a doctor told him that he had a serious, if not fatal, case of tuberculosis and that he needed rest and good nourishment. Returning to Pagoda Anchorage, he spent the next four months rapidly deteriorating, despite the care provided for him by Miss Barber and the students at her school. "For two months, I lived daily in the very jaws of Satan," he wrote.[38] Nevertheless, his condition improved at the very point when hope was lost, and he started writing his book *The Spiritual Man*. His recovery was slow and not miraculous. The disease persisted for at least three years. Lee's book tells us that Watchman Nee became sick with tuberculosis in his lungs in 1924. Later in the book we read, "While Brother Nee was seriously sick with tuberculosis, his heart was stricken with angina pectoris in 1927." How sick was he? Lee's biography tell us that he had been active:

> In November of 1924, he visited Sitiawan in Malaysia. He visited Sitiawan in Malaysia. He visited the same place the following year and established the first church in Southeast Asia. He returned to China from Malaysia in May 1925."[39]

This was quite consistent with the tuberculosis: "Dormant but viable organisms persist for years, and reactivation of disease in any of these sites may occur if the host's defense mechanisms become impaired."[40] It is probably certain that Nee had the disease. His descriptions of his illness fit perfectly. Photos of him at this time show the symptomatic weight loss. There are also times during a patient's illness when he feels healthy enough to make trips to other countries as Watchman Nee did. Tuberculosis was quite common at that time in Asia. What Nee did not know was that during the times he worked in Malaysia, he could infect others.

After recovering a portion of his health, Nee returned to Shanghai to seek the literary assistance of his friend Ruth Lee, who had been a teacher in a Nanking college. There, Lee introduced Nee to Peace Wang, the daughter of a wealthy magistrate. At the Wang home Nee, Lee, Wang, and Charles Judd, an accountant with the interdenominational China Inland Mission, met in a manner like the early church, when it was the custom of believers to meet in homes. This group in 1927 became the first Christian "assembly place" founded on Nee's principle of locality.

From there, the work quickly spread, and many local churches were founded. The rapid success of Nee's indigenous church movement was due to a number of factors: anti-Western feelings in China during the 1920s and 1930s; interdenominational rivalries, which disheartened many faithful natives; the rise of the indigenous church movement in its varied forms;* and the church's neglect of the spiritual aspect of Christianity in its deference to agrarian and educational programs. But certainly Nee's gifted preaching

---

* Peter S. Goertz in his Ph.D. dissertation, "A History of the Chinese Indigenous Christian Church under the American Board in Fukien Province" (Yale University, 1933), pp. 5-6, lists the four prevailing opinions of the meaning of indigenous church:

1. Those most antiwestern in sentiment preferred a church whose founder was a native Oriental.

2. Many Westerners felt that those churches already in China are indigenous by their very nature despite its financial or organizational manner.

3. The London Missionary Society early in the nineteenth century developed the three-self concept. Its idea of self-supporting, self-governing and self-propagating became the official policy of the Chinese Communist government.

4. The American Methodist Church believed in an indigenous church in a national sense. The church was to be "ground in Chinese soul" but could have outside authority.

and teaching, and the real sense of brotherhood expressed by the "Little Flock" congregations* were also responsible.

As has been described earlier, Nee had had some contact with the "London Group" of Brethren. This relationship was strengthened by the visit of a certain Mr. Charles Barlow in December 1930. Upon his return to England he relayed to a number of churches his absolute joy at meeting fellow Christians in China who had independently concluded that Brethren doctrine was basically correct. Correspondence between the two groups led to a visitation in October of 1932 of eight London Brethren. At first cautious in breaking bread with the Chinese congregation, they finally concluded that mutual fellowship was entirely consistent with their exclusivism.

In the spring of that year, Nee received an invitation from Barlow to speak in England and America. Upon his arrival at Peterborough, England, Nee discovered that an elaborate speaking plan had been set up that limited his teaching opportunities to Brethren groups. Sensing that his hosts were too exclusive to permit him fellowship with non-Brethren, Nee told Barlow that he had to go to London for a week on "business." While the Brethren assumed his trip to be nonreligious, Nee's business was the Lord's. He went to the independent, evangelical Christian Fellowship Centre in Honor Oak Road, South London. T. Austin-Sparks, its head pastor and a favorite writer of Nee, was absent, but Nee did take the opportunity to break bread with the assistant pastor, George Patterson.

Beginning at the English docks, his American engagement was escorted by James Taylor, Sr., a Brooklyn, New York,

---

* Many cults and religious movements have capitalized on the apparent disparity between the biblical concept of fellowship and its practice in the modern church (viz., Jehovah's Witnesses, Mormons, Jesus People, charismatic movement).

Brethren leader. Barlow's enthusiasm for Nee and the "Little Flock" was not shared by Taylor. During the ocean voyage Nee expressed to him many of his own teachings on certain doctrines. To Taylor, the eclectic pattern of his teachings was in serious error. Upon his arrival in New York, Nee gave a sermon (on deliverance), which Taylor felt was deficient doctrinally. By the time Nee had reached China, a more serious charge had been brought by Taylor. He had discovered, quite by accident, that Nee had fellowship with non-Brethren. The Brethren quickly broke off relationships with the Chinese congregations and its leader.

Nee had also become disenchanted by their "spiritual pride," and likened them to the Laodicean Church in the Book of Revelation.[41] In his typically anthropological manner, he criticized them for "their excessive stress of the objective truth [perfection in Christ] and neglect of the subjective truth [the ongoing, inner work of the Holy Spirit]." [42]

The Brethren were too objective, whereas the Chinese Pentecostal movement suffered from an excessive subjectivity, according to Nee. Its emphasis on power, Nee felt, was regrettable. In a booklet first published in 1933, he warned others "to discern in a meeting if a person's power is psychical or spiritual."[43] Personally, he did not oppose speaking in tongues and in 1935 became involved with the movement through the mission of Miss Elizabeth Fischbacher of the China Inland Mission.

At that time, she began to counsel Nee, who was seeking further spiritual power to overcome many missionary frustrations. In spite of his fundamental reservation to the instruction of men by women, he found peace and spiritual blessing in her message and some experiences associated with her Pentecostal theology.

"I have met the Lord," he wrote shortly afterwards. But did Nee himself speak in tongues? Witness Lee, in his small booklet *The Baptism in the Holy Spirit*, writes:

> Brother Nee has never spoken in tongues. Once he sent me a cable with only the words: "Not all speak in tongues." He has studied the Word very thoroughly. I have never met a man so well versed in the scripture as he. He has found it unmistakenly clear that "not all speak in tongues." To insist all must speak in tongues is unscriptural, but to say that speaking in tongues is dispensationally over is also wrong."[44]

What Mr. Lee has said conveys quite well Watchman Nee's own feelings. In his books on biblical psychology, he warned others against ecstatic religious experiences related to the animal elements of the human *psuchë*, which does not produce resurrection life (*zöë*).[45] Mrs. Carol Stearns, one of Nee's closest non-Oriental friends who lived in China, in an interview agreed that Nee never spoke in tongues.[46]

Nee saw in Mrs. Fischbacher and other Pentecostals a real personal faith in Jesus Christ. He never regarded speaking in tongues as unbiblical, but he did react to many of the excesses that accompany charismatic worship.[47] According to Mrs. Stearns, Nee prayed to God that He would not give him the gift of tongues, because he did not want to be identified with the Pentecostals in the South.*

During the time of Nee's close association with Mrs. Fischbacher, Keswick theology became a more influential part of his theological teaching. In fact, with Fischbacher's assistance, Nee attended the 1938 Keswick Convention. In

---

* Stearns, interview. The Pentecostal movement arrived in China in 1907. In that year, Nettie Moomau, a participant in the Azusa Street Revival in Los Angeles, started a revival in Hong Kong that eventually reached the southern provinces of Kwangtung, Kwangsi, and Yunnan. From that time onward, the South represented a center of denominational Pentecostalism.[48]

its commemorative volume, Nee was remembered for uttering a prayer for peace between China and Japan.[49] It was during and after his visit to England and other European countries that the addresses contained in Nee's most popular volume, *The Normal Christian Life*, were given. At the center of this book's ideas is the exegesis of Romans 7 according to the Keswick Movement.[50]

There was another woman in Nee's life as well. He married his adolescent sweetheart Charity Chang. He had known her for ten years. Some of that time she had been an unbelieving critic of the idea of God. She even ridiculed the idea of God. God saved her and delivered her from at least her spirit of unbelief. They were married in 1934 and Witness Lee served as a sort of best man.

The Little Flock and the Revolution

From the beginning of his active ministry, Nee shared with many of the Chinese Communist leaders a distrust of the organizational system of Protestant and Catholic missions— its wealth, its dependence upon foreign resources, and its hierarchical structure. If any church or mission were so well established that its workers received salaries, that a building for worship was constructed and maintained, that charitable funds were available in reserve, and that fund raising was organized and institutionalized, how could it trust in the Lord for its needs? If a worker in the church, such as Nee, had been under salary, he would have had "his hope in men." When their resources dried up, his resources would have dried up, too.[51] But while the Communists innately rejected any form of Christianity and placed their trust in a new political system, Nee proposed a new *ekklesia* dependent upon the Lord for its needs.

During a conference held in 1938 in Shanghai and Hankow, he delivered a series of messages to "the inner circle of my [Nee's] most intimate associates in the work," in which he examined the biblical teaching on the church and its expression in his own ministry.[52] As for the minister's financial needs, Nee said, "... there are evidently two ways by which the needs of God's servants may be met—either they look to God to touch the hearts of His children to give what is needful, or they can earn it by doing part-time 'secular' work."[53] The latter method Nee considered as an option "in special circumstances."

According to the biographies of Angus Kinnear and Witness Lee, Nee left the place of leadership to help the material needs of the believers. In 1942 commercial trade outside of China had been nearly eliminated by the Japanese occupation of the eastern seaboard. Finances within unoccupied China were limited. Feeling that the church should not be burdened with providing him with material needs, he accepted an invitation to help in the administration of his brother George's chemical factory. The job provided income for himself and other Christians he hired, and it may have served as one means of overcoming his professional boredom as a result of twenty-two years of church work.[54]

The company, CBC Laboratories, expanded as wartime needs for sulfanilamide, its chief product, increased, and Nee's work there became full time. There is a bit of mystery here. It is not quite clear whether he left the church on his own or was under pressure to leave. He was apparently generous helping people with the company funds, and yet, fellow Christians in the factory were unhappy with him. Lee says, "Satan stirred up turmoil among the saints in Shanghai against Watchman."[55] The elders at the Hardoon Road, Shanghai assembly asked him to stop preaching until he had given up his job. Nee was facing some serious problems. Someone was embezzling money from the company. As manager of the company, he should have known what was going on.* This brief association with capitalism and his subsequent "turning over" of the factory to the church would bring the "Little Flock" in disfavor with the Communist authorities after the fall of the Kuomin-tang.

In 1938 Nee told his fellow workers:

> It is perfectly in order for one or more members of a church to run a hospital or a school or to be responsible for mission-work, but not for any church as a whole. A church exists for the purpose of mutual help in one place, not for the purpose of bearing responsibility of work in different places. According to God's Word, all the work is the personal concern of individual brothers called and commissioned by God, as members of the Body, and not the concern of any church as a body. The responsibility of the work is always borne by one or more individuals.[57]

If institutions of social welfare were excluded from church control, it was even truer of profitable enterprises. Is this the reason that the elders of the church in Shanghai asked him to stop serving? We don't know the answer. The elders involved in the decision remain silent. There were rumors. His friend and co-worker Witness Lee was well aware of them when he published his long-awaited biography in 1991. The book, *Watchman Nee: A Seer of the Divine Revelation in the Present Age* is more a systematic defense of Watchman Nee's life and character. "A rumor is nothing but a lie," Lee says.[58] Lee does not tell us what the rumors were, but one has to wonder why he tells us about Watchman Nee's marriage to Charity in 1934 and then tells us about his work in business in 1942. It seems to be an odd connection until you understand what the rumors were.

---

* C.T. Chan's study of his uncle gives us an anecdotal description of the factory (financial difficulties and intra-company embezzlement) and Watchman's personality (in the face of business pressure) during this five-year interim in Nee's ministry.[56]

A Question of Character

Recently a book published in Hong Kong called into question the character of Watchman Nee himself. What is most troubling is that it comes from the personal diaries of one of China's greatest Christians, Wang Ming Dao. Back in 1981, I heard allegations that Watchman Nee's absence from the ministry was not about being busy with business. There were rumors of adultery. When I asked an elder Chinese Christian who had attended his church about the allegations, his answer was a vague, "There were problems." It was an uncomfortable subject for those inside and outside his movement. If it happened, the people who know the truth are dead now. It may or may not be true.

It's not the first time that a great, spiritual leader has been entangled in the world. It seems that every time there's someone we see as spiritual and a great leader, he has a downfall. The leader must accept responsibility. Christians must avoid becoming gossip mongers. Christians must also stop exalting a member of the body of Christ as "a seer," "the man of the hour," "the greatest" or anything else.

In the divine plan, Paul was greater than Watchman Nee. Yet, the exorbitant praise by the people of Lystra was unspiritual:

> "Men, why are you doing this? We too are only men, human like you. We are bringing you good news, telling you to turn from these worthless things to the living God, who made heaven and earth and sea and everything in them. In the past, he let all nations go their own way. Yet he has not left himself without testimony: He has shown kindness by giving you rain from heaven and crops in their seasons; he provides you with plenty of food and fills your hearts with joy. Even with these words, they had difficulty keeping the crowd from sacrificing to them" (Acts 14:15-18).

In the church at Corinth was too much praise for the Super Apostles. Paul had to remind them of something quite simple: the power of God:

"Brothers, think of what you were when you were called. Not many of you were wise by human standards; not many were influential; not many were of noble birth. But God chose the foolish things of the world to shame the wise; God chose the weak things of the world to shame the strong. He chose the lowly things of this world and the despised things—and the things that are not—to nullify the things that are, so that no one may boast before him. It is because of him that you are in Christ Jesus, who has become for us wisdom from God—that is, our righteousness, holiness and redemption. Therefore, as it is written: 'Let him who boasts boast in the Lord'" (1 Cor. 1:26-31).

Of course, there is King David. In a sermon given by Paul, he says, "After removing Saul, he made David their king. He [God] testified concerning him: I have found David son of Jesse a man after my own heart; he will do everything I want him to do." You know who David was: an adulterer and a murderer.

The language in the Angus Kinnear's biography and even more so in Witness Lee's account is so spiritual that Watchman Nee appears angelic and unnatural. Can you imagine what it is like to be such a Super Christian? You can't make mistakes as Moses did. You always have to have a spiritual answer. You can't answer a question with an honest, "Gee, I don't know." You can't yawn when someone speaks. Friendship must always look "spiritual." You can't have any personal, natural choices or favorites in the categories of people, children, foods, dogs, or cats.

If you are married, your wife and children are likely to be skeptical or distant. Everything you do is a spiritual lesson. Under such a fishbowl life, many great pastors turn to a secret life to feel happy and human. It's as though they are so exalted that they have to get down in the mud to feel fully human.

It's hard to believe, but two of the evangelical churches where I once worshipped had pastors who were secret alcoholics and transvestites. Both churches regarded these fallen men as the "most anointed pastors they had ever had."

Nee and all the assemblies also believed that those churches founded by the apostles are based upon the ground of locality. They are "intensely local," and in organization, "the churches are totally independent of one another." Only spiritually are they "one" and interdependent as the true church.[59]*

In 1947 Nee was no longer a leader in the local church movement or in the Shanghai assembly. The Local Church as a movement had been reestablished by a former bookstore worker, Witness Lee. Feeling the call of God and desiring to build upon an everlasting kingdom, Nee returned to the church that year. As for the factory that he now managed, he saw it as an opportunity to provide for the work of the church. Nee consigned all the property to the church. His actions were contrary to his teachings of 1938. By this action, Nee quickly returned to a place of favor in the flock and began to preach and teach.

The preaching emphasis changed after 1947. Where once the basis of unity among the brethren was symbolized by the phrase, "breaking of bread," it was now demonstrated by the "handing over" principle. The church no longer could say, "Silver and gold have I none," for now the church owned factories that had been turned over by its members to the control of the elders chosen from the congregation. Ecclesiastical structure changed as the work and its workers, instead of locality, became the foundation of authority. The doctrinal reversal was systematized in the "Jerusalem principle" established in February of 1948. First suggested by Lee, this plan called for the founding of missionary centers in Foochow and other large cities that would send out a host of workers to one area as a form of saturation evangelism.

---

* For a more complete summary and evaluation of Nee's ecclesiology, see chapter 5.

Nee's popularity rose dramatically, but others dissented from the church's change of emphasis. Nee's own nephew became disillusioned by the growing idolization of Watchman.[60] Lyall even reports that the clicking that accompanied Nee's speech because of his loose-fitting dentures was often unconsciously imitated in prayer.[61]*

As the period of religious freedom was drawing to an end, the places of assembly expanded dramatically. As their own numbers dwindled, denominational leaders expressed divided opinion on the Christian witness of the movement. Patterson and Wang[62] agreed that its members' "love for God and for each other sets a wonderful example."[63] Notson and Paton[64] were far less sympathetic and depicted them as heretical or "helplessly subject to the manipulation" of its leaders.[65] But both felt that the rise of the movement reflected the denominational churches' own shortcomings. Paton, an Anglican, wrote, "It is a tragedy that catholic order and the freedom of the Spirit were ever opposed to each other; and it would not have happened if we had not exported to China our torn and mutilated Western postmedieval Christian tradition."[66]

Nee's Imprisonment

Much has been written in the past few years in Christian literature concerning Watchman Nee's imprisonment and death. Since the purpose of this book is to examine the direction and origins of specific teachings, it is not necessary to repeat a detailed account of the historical events. Certain facts are, however, significant in an evaluation of the success and future of Nee's teachings.

---

* I observed a similar phenomenon among the older Chinese Christians who attended the assembly in Hollis, New York, that was founded by Nee's associate, Stephen Kaung.

On October 1, 1949, Mao Tse-tung declared the establishment of the People's Republic of China. The Koumintang government, sympathetic to Christian missions, had fled, and for those Christians who remained in their homeland, it was a time of immense tension, as described by an eyewitness:

> That first summer was a strange time. Business was almost at a standstill. We were cut off from the outside world. The once crowded harbor was almost empty, and the streets had not half of their previous traffic. Yet, daily life went on with not so many outward changes. For some reason the Communists did not interfere with life in Shanghai nearly so much or so soon as in smaller towns and in the country. People coming into the city from the interior would say: "Oh, you have not been properly liberated yet. You can still do what you like, you are almost free!"
>
> … A feeling of tension was kept up by the constant reports of mass arrests and executions; and almost daily one saw truckloads of wretched men and women, crouching on the floor, being hurried away to judgment.[67]

Yet, in the assembly places the "work" continued. Teaching seminars became the central concern of Nee's own ministry, in order to equip the saints for the difficulties ahead.

When accusation meetings were convened under government direction in the Christian assemblies, it became evident that policies and practices within the Little Flock had made the organization vulnerable to anti-imperialistic campaigns. The September 30, 1951, issue of the Communist *Tien Feng Magazine* reported the beginning of accusation meetings against the church and particularly against its leader, Watchman Nee, as an imperialist.

Nee sensed that the end was near and spent almost all his time preparing studies. Proofs on the existence of God and practical studies on the nature of Christ's righteousness, the wisdom and glory of God that is inherited by the believer, and the power of Christ's resurrection were dictated to Ruth Lee and two assistants.[68] When the Communists took over Shanghai, Nee studied extensively the writings of Marx and Engels for a month, and in a series of lectures, he openly told the congregation that the Marxist system was shallow compared to the perfection of Christ and was incompatible with Christian ideals.[69] But cooperation with the new government on the lines of Romans 13, he taught, was within the character of the normal Christian life.[70] His last instruction to the church was to nullify its association with business, saying: "Tell them in Hong Kong to disassociate all secular business enterprise from the church."[71] But the command came too late.

After being ordered out of Shanghai, he was arrested in Manchuria by the Department of Public Safety on April 10, 1952. He was charged with participating in five corrupt business practices. On January 18, 1956, as part of its plan to destroy the open meetings of the Little Flock, Nee was further charged with activities hostile to government policies, financial irregularities, and multiple counts of adultery. The charges of capitalism were specified at that time and included bribing tax officials, stealing state secrets, and having unauthorized contracts in Hong Kong and in Taiwan with the "bandit Chiang."[72] On April 12, 1952, Nee began serving a fifteen-year sentence. With its leader in prison, the assembly of Shanghai excommunicated Nee, and those continuing to worship within the assembly buildings joined the Three-Self Movement. The rest of the church went underground and survived the Cultural Revolution that saw the end of outward expressions of worship.

Contrary to reports of torture and mutilation, Nee was given a sufficient diet to serve the state as a translator of

English chemical journals. In May 1968, a Red Chinese official requested political asylum. He told authorities that while serving as a prison guard in Shanghai, Watchman Nee had converted him to Jesus Christ.[73] If his statement is true, it testifies to Nee's faithfulness to his Christian hope. On June 1, 1972, four years later, Watchman Nee died and received the reward for his patience and suffering.

Some have speculated that his death was not from natural causes. His death, they postulate, occurred as the result of President Nixon's trip to China in February of 1972. During the trip, someone asked a Chinese official about the condition of Watchman Nee. It is theorized that in order to avoid further embarrassment, the government executed him and reported his death from a heart attack.

It is true that a number of Christian reporters accompanied the president to China, and one of the Christian newsmen, acting as their representative, did ask a Chinese representative about Nee.* But in 1972 Nee was in very ill health. He was sixty-nine years old and suffered from a heart condition. In addition to prison conditions.[74†] Nee had despaired over the recent death of his wife. In a letter dated May 22, 1972, he wrote to his sister-in-law that he was in ill health, but that nevertheless his "inward joy" surpassed everything.[75] The evidence for any political execution seems circumstantial. If this were the case, the responsibility for such an action would rest totally upon the Chinese and not with the reporter.

What was it like for Watchmen Nee during his long imprisonment? His letters were censored. He could not talk

---

* As was the custom, the official changed the subject and avoided any further discussiion on the matter. Emett C. McKowen, U. S. Information Agency to Dana Roberts, December 12, 1975.

† Nee spent twenty years at Shanghai First Municipal Prison. In April 1972, Nee was transferred to an open center further inland. For a description of prison conditions see n. [74]

about his Lord in letters. His wife Charity was allowed to visit him until her death in 1971. What things did he learn from God? Did he have any regrets? We don't know. After he died a note was found under his pillow. It read,

> Christ is the Son of God who died for the redemption of sinners and resurrected after three days. This is the greatest truth in the universe. I die because of my belief in Christ.[76]

Work of Nee's Followers

The weight and character of Nee's teachings are evident in the Little Flock in and out of China. In China the movement survives because of its religious roots independent of a hierarchical structure in which a government might attempt to impose its own will. Unlike many of the denominations in China at the time, it was grounded upon an inner life where the heart seeks a life in God.

In *Further Talks on the Church Life* Nee discovered in the Book of Acts a method of evangelism where a representative part of the church migrated to another area.* When the Little Flock was forced to leave the city and find refuge in the countryside or outside of China, the church saw the persecution as an opportunity to evangelize unreached areas.

Outside of China the Little Flock Movement grew openly through local evangelism and a publishing ministry. In Asia its members are found in most Chinese settlements. Parading in the streets in "gospel shirts" decorated with Bible passages colored green, they have called others to believe: "Who will accept Jesus? Who will do the Lord's work?"[78] In America and

---

* "Whether a migration is peaceful or due to persecution, it is nevertheless a migration. The way of Jerusalem is to migrate; the only difference is that they went out because of persecution."[77]

England a number of assemblies have been established—based upon Nee's principles of locality, authority by a group of elders without a pastor/ rector, unstructured charismatic worship, and evangelism—through the sending out of "workers" or by the distribution of books to Christians by Nee or his two fellow workers, Witness Lee and Stephen Kaung.

Stephen Kaung, a former worker in Chungking, fled China with a number of Little Flock members and established an assembly in Hollis, New York, a section of the borough of Queens. When I visited them in 1973, the assembly was of Chinese, Spanish, and English descent. Its serviced included singing, extemporaneous prayer, meditation upon Scripture in which members openly reflected upon its meaning,* a sermon delivered by one of the church elders, the "Lord's Supper" with a common cup, and a concluding "Love Feast" of food reflecting the international quality of the congregation.

Unlike Nee's original teachings, they do not consider their church as the only true church in the area. The church has no name by its doors, simply called by the believers, "the assembly hall," in order that its name may not serve as a basis of division from other churches.

In keeping with its teachings on missions, the church has "sent out" Rev. Kaung to minister in the Washington, D.C., area. There Kaung assisted in the building up of another congregation, led Bible classes for a chapter of the Full Gospel Business Men's Fellowship,† wrote books, and continues the work of translating Watchman Nee's teachings into English.

---

* See Nee's teachings on the ministry of the Word in chapter 3.

† Established in 1953 by dairy businessman Demos Shakarian, the Full Gospel Business Men's Fellowship International is an interdenominational organization, which promotes the Pentecostal experience through banquets, luncheons, and conventions in a manner appealing to "blue and white collar" workers.[79]

Kaung's present publications and his many audio sermons available on the Internet testify to the influence on his exegetical style of his former teacher and senior co-worker, Watchman Nee. In *The Song of Degrees*, Psalms 120-34 are taken as an occasion to describe the progressive "ascent of the soul," which leads to the believer's unity with God the Father. Beginning with Psalm 125, believers "begin to perceive that within ourselves there is that which is of the Spirit and that which is of the flesh."[80] The strategy and victory herein described is similar to that given by Nee in *The Spiritual Man* and *The Release of the Spirit*.

In *The Splendor of His Ways*, the Book of Job is interpreted in similar anthropological language. All four of Job's earthly counselors are understood as both outward and inward representations of our religious consciousness, even though he believes the narration to be a historical account.

	Outward	Inward
Eliphaz[81]	mysticism	emotion of the soul
Bildad[82]	traditionalism	mind of the soul
Zophar[83]	dogmatism	will of the soul
Elihu[84]	spiritual life	human spirit

Thus, anthropological concerns predominate in Kaung's teachings and give further testimony to the significance of the concept of man in Nee's theology.

Witness Lee (1905-1997)

Much of the controlling leadership of the Little Flock Movement came into in the hands of another of Nee's colleagues, Witness Lee. From his position as an elder in a newly formed Taiwan local church congregation in 1951, his authority has grown to include twenty-six churches in the United States and numerous local churches in Germany,

England, Korea, the Philippines, New Zealand, and Hong Kong. His leadership and teaching have come under some sharp criticism from people within and outside of the local church phenomenon.

James Mo-Oi Cheung, in his book *The Ecclesiology of Watchman Nee and Witness Lee*, accused Lee of unorthodox teachings.[85] A few months after its first printing in 1972, the book was removed from the market when it was discovered that Cheung had made some serious errors in his thesis. Watchman Nee's book, *The Glorious Church*, had been wrongly assigned to the authorship of Witness Lee.[86] An extensive appendix containing spurious or unsubstantiated statements about Lee had been used as a resource to interpret the state of Lee's heterodoxy.[87] Cheung's contrast between Nee and Lee was therefore somewhat invalidated by the research inexactness.

In a series of four articles in *Nan Pei Chi*, a Hong Kong news magazine, comparable in style and popularity to that of *Newsweek*, two anonymous writers gave an extensive account of certain irregularities in the work of a Little Flock leader identified by subterfuge as Wit X Lee.[88] In the serial, Lee is accused of:

> 1. Political and economic activities, which were the basis of Nee's imprisonment.

> 2. Using Nee's greatness to foster his own religious kingdom in Asia and in the United States.

> 3. Taking Christians to civil court (contrary to 1 Corinthians 6:1-11) in order to gain control of a congregation and its church property.

While it is perhaps difficult to prove the first allegation, and the second is merely an interpretation of motives, the events of the conspiracy described in the article are well-known facts in Hong Kong as the result of newspaper publicity.

Such activities are certainly in sharp contrast to the submissive nature associated with the name of Watchman Nee,* and it is indeed a pity that many in Asia and America see him as the spiritual and intellectual successor to Watchman Nee.

The Internet and the news report that many Local Churches have taken criticism to courts. While most of the time the judges have supported their lawsuits, they may have lost the publicity wars. Christians read:

> "So then, men ought to regard us as servants of Christ and as those entrusted with the secret things of God. Now it is required that those who have been given a trust must prove faithful. I care very little if I am judged by you or by any human court; indeed, I do not even judge myself. My conscience is clear, but that does not make me innocent. It is the Lord who judges me. Therefore judge nothing before the appointed time; wait till the Lord comes. He will bring to light what is hidden in darkness and will expose the motives of men's hearts. At that time each will receive his praise from God" (1 Cor. 4:1-5, See also James 4:6-7).

> If any of you has a dispute with another, dare he take it before the ungodly for judgment instead of before the saints? Do you not know that the saints will judge the world? And if you are to judge the world, are you not competent to judge trivial cases? (1 Cor. 6:1-2).

Perhaps the most Damaging to Lee's position as a Christian leader comes from his own book, *Watchman Nee: A Seer of the Divine Revelation in the Present Age*. After I read this book, I was less sympathetic to Watchman Nee

---

* In *The Normal Christian Church Life*, Nee writes: "When an apostle comes to a place where a local church already exists, he must never forget that no church authority rests with him. Should he desire to work in a place where the local church does not wish to have him, then all he can do is to pass on to some other part" (p. 80). Nee readily accepted such church decisions in his own ministry.

and embarrassed at reading Brother Lee's effort to exalt his own position within the body of Christ.

Among the American churches, Lee's authority is not evident in any form of monarchial system of ecclesiology in which he serves as the chief apostle or archbishop. It is much more subtle than that. Each church has a number of teaching elders (as they see it), according to God's dispensation of charisms. The congregation outwardly recognizes this by their harmonious shouts of "Amen!" and "Hallelujah!" during the delivery of his Bible exposition or sermon. Despite their strong assertions to the contrary, much of the content and form of these "inspired teachings" comes from reading Nee's and Lee's books. When Lee was still living, most, if not all, of the elders attended one of his "training" sessions. Here they receive intensified instruction on interpreting a portion of Scripture by one's "spirit-reading"* of the Bible. Since Lee is the best interpreter of Nee's teachings and the Bible, diversity is difficult. In one meeting, I asked an elder if he reads anything on the Bible other than the writings of Nee and Lee. He replied, "Yes, you mean Jessie Penn-Lewis. Some of us read her books."

"But what about Christian writers like Wesley, F.F. Bruce, Schaeffer, or even Thomas à Kempis?" I asked.

"We cannot be sure about these people," he replied. "Why should we read them if we already have the truth?"

By his remarks this elder demonstrates the all-encompassing influence of Nee and Lee's instruction on anthropology.[89] Since both men have shown the proper way of determining what insights are of the human spirit enlightened by the Holy Spirit and what are of the soul,

---

* See chapter 3 for Nee's teachings on the ministry of the Word.

other books are "mixed" products—among their inspired insights there are soulish, unspiritual elements.

But Lee's messages lack much of the polish and intellectual care so typical of Nee's writings. On Gal. 1:4, Lee writes:

> Many Bible translators translate the Greek word for *age* into *world*, because an age is a part or period of the whole world. All the ages added together equal the world. During the time of the Apostle Paul, there was a certain age. If you have ever read the world history of that period of time, you could see that the age had three aspects: Greek philosophy, Roman politics, and the Hebrew religion. The Greeks brought in the philosophy, the wisdom, and the knowledge. The Romans brought in the way to govern and organize a strong administration. Then the Hebrews had the best religion. Now we can see that what Paul means when he speaks of the present evil age is the Hebrew religion.[90]

But if someone were to interject that such an interpretation is inconsistent with the biblical usage of *aiön*,[91] those adhering to Lee's theology would reply that such an objection is according to religion and not according to Christ:

> Religion, politics, the faith, and scriptural interpretation must all pass away for us. Christ has the answer to each of these questions, but he does not care for; neither must we care for anything but the living Lord, the living Christ. As long as we have His presence, it is sufficient. We must learn just to turn to our spirit and say, O Lord! This is the way to experience Him.[92]

> ... When I was young I did much searching and researching of the Bible. But, Hallelujah, today I have given it up ...[93]

The mark of this Christocentrism in today's "Small Flock" or "local church" congregations is rather vague in Lee's books, but it appears to be interrelated with his dogmatic assertions about the need for all believers to see the doctrine of locality, to say "Amen" and "Hallelujah" in the congregational worship, and to be able to discern between soul and spirit. Like Nee and Kaung, biblical anthropology according to a trichotomous division plays an important part in his theology. Avoidance of objective methods of biblical study and an outright denial of evangelical hermeneutics[94] has caused Lee to accept unorthodox ritual within his local churches. He writes:

> In the beginning of 1968, something really happened in Los Angeles. The burial. It was the time of the New Year Conference, and I had no intention of encouraging people to be buried. But at the closing of one meeting, one said, "I want to be buried," then others followed until many brothers and sisters in the church were buried. They were all so deeply moved to testify by this act that they were burying all their oldness, and by doing this they became alive. I was really surprised by this move to be buried. I was trying, in fact, to say some word to stop it, but I was checked by the Spirit within. Who was I to stop something of the Holy Spirit? I said not a word until the third day, when I predicted that the church in Los Angeles would certainly be criticized by the religious people for this act. It was not more than ten days before the criticism came. "There is heresy in Los Angeles," they said. "Believers who are already properly baptized are being baptized again. Where is the scriptural ground for a believer to be baptized again after being properly baptized already?" I do not like to argue, but I wish to tell you that so many withered "hands" were healed. Not only did this occur in Los Angeles, but followed this in many places, many dead ones through this kind of burial came alive. What can we say?[95]

Are Lee's assemblies heretical? Clearly it has many of the characteristics of "heresy" described both by Schlier and Farrer[96]—lack of love toward fellow believers, self-assertiveness, a self-chosen authority of a teacher, and an authoritative stand on a disputable doctrine(s) (e.g., repeated baptisms, ecclesiology, tripartite anthropology, and biblical interpretation). As will be seen in the following chapters, Lee's experiential hermeneutics, doctrinal laissez-faire, and absolute exclusiveness are less in keeping with the theological balance presented in the content of the entire literary production of Watchman Nee.

Chapter 1 Endnotes

1. Marcel Girard, ed., *Nagel's Encyclopedia-Guide*: China (Geneva: Nagel Publications, 1968), p. 1157.

2. Edmund J. Wehrle, *Britain, China and the Anti-missionary Riots, 1891-1900* (Minneapolis: University of Minnesota, 1966), p. ix.

3. Robert Philip, *Peace with China! or, The Crisis of Christianity in Central Asia: A Letter to the Right Honourable T.B. Macauly, Secretary at War.* (London: John Snow, 1840), p. 4.

4. Tang Tse-Shing, *Death Blow to Corrupt Doctrines: A Plain Statement of Facts* (Shanghai: The Gentry and People, 1870), p. 13.

5. Peter S. Goertz, "A History of the Chinese Indigenous Christian Church under the American Board in Fukien Province" (Ph.D. dissertation, Yale University, 1933), p. 165.

6. Rev. R. Anderson to S.F. Woodin, December 31, 1863, American Board of Missions, Foochow Missionaries Document Vol. 301, Harvard University, Cambridge, Mass. Angus Kinnear [*The Story of Watchman Nee: Against the Tide* (Fort Washington, Pa.: Christian Literature Crusade, 1973), p. 20.] is incorrect in saying that U-Cheng was the first to be ordained. Mission records show that Ding Long-Go was ordained on April 23, 1876, one month earlier than Nga U-Cheng. Anderson to Woodin, June 30, 1876.

7. Kinnear, *Against the Tide*, p. 23. The quote is not cited in his notes, but it is probably from Nee Lin Ho-P'ing, *En Ai Piao Pen* [An Object of Grace and Love] (Shanghai, 1943).

8. Juvenal 6. 602; Lactantius *The Divine Institutes* bk. 6. 20; Tertullian *Ad Nationes* 15.

9. W.S. Packenham-Welsh, *Twenty Years in China* (Cambridge: W. Heffer & Sons Ltd., 1935), p. 95.

10. Packenham-Welsh, *Twenty Years*, p. 5.

11. Watchman Nee, *Watchman Nee's Testimony*, comp. K.H. Weigh (Hong Kong: Church Book Room Ltd., 1974), pp. 11-12.

12. A contemporary account is given in Edward Thomas Williams, *A Short History of China* (New York: Harper & Brothers, 1928), pp. 324f, 353, 372, 653.

13. There is a disparity of accounts concerning the date of Miss Yu's revival meeting. In Leslie T. Lyall's *Three of China's Mighty Men* [(London: Overseas Missionary Fellowship, 1973), p. 52] the date is set at the end of 1919; in Kinnear's *Against the Tide* (pp. 32-33), at the end of February 1920; in *Watchman Nee's Testimony* (p. 10), April of the same year; and both C.T. Chan's *My Uncle Watchman Nee* [Wo-Ti Kau Fu Nee To-Sheng (Hong Kong: The Alliance Press, 1970), p. 7] and James Mo-Oi Cheung's *The Ecclesiology of Watchman Nee and Witness Lee* [(Fort Washington, Pa.: Christian Literature Crusade, 1972), pp. 14-15] as late as 1922. Cheung and Chan have apparently confused the events of Nee's conversion with that of his "baptism in the Holy Spirit."

14. Kinnear, *Against the Tide*, p. 33.

15. Ibid., p. 34.

16. Nee, Testimony, p. 10.

17. Watchman Nee, *A Living Sacrifice*, Basic Lesson Series, vol. 1 [trans. Stephen Kaung] (New York: Christian Fellowship Publishers, Inc., 1972), p. 30.

18. Idem, *The Spiritual Man*, 3 vols. [trans. Stephen Kaung] (New York: Christian Fellowship Publishers, Inc., 1968), 1:88-89.

19. Idem, *Testimony*, p. 12.

20. Nee, *Testimony*, p. 15.

21. Ibid., p. 17-18.

22. Witness Lee, *Watchman Nee; A Seer of the Divine Revelation in the Present Age* (Anaheim, Ca: Living Stream Ministry, 1991), p. 38, 54.

23. Nee. *Testimony*, p. 25.

24. Ibid., p. 24.

25. Rom. 6:3; Mark 16:16; Nee, *The Good Confession*, Basic Lesson Series, vol. 2 [trans. Stephen Kaung] (New York: Christian Fellowship Publishers, Inc., 1973), pp. 21-22; idem, *Living Sacrifice*, p. 13.

26. Lyall, *Mighty Men*, p. 56.

27. Kinnear, *Against the Tide*, pp. 48, 78.

28. For a history of these two events see Steven Barabas, *So Great Salvation: The History of the Keswick Convention* (London: Marshall, Morgan & Scott, 1952); David Matthews, *I Saw the Welsh Revival* (Chicago, Moody Press, 1951); Rev. J. Vyrnwy Moran, *The Welsh Religious Revival 1904-5: A Retrospect and a Criticism* (London: Chapman & Hall Ltd., 1909); Jessie Penn-Lewis, *The Awakening in Wales* (Dorset, England: The Overcomer Literature Trust, n.d.); John Pollock, "A Hundred Years of Keswick," *Christianity Today*, June 20, 1975, pp. 6-8; and G. Campbell Morgan and W.T. Stead, *The Welsh Revival* (Boston: The Pilgrim Press, 1905).

29. Lee, *Nee*, p. 23.

30. Idem, *The Centrality of the Cross* (Dorset, England: The Overcomer Literature Trust, n.d.), pp. 7, 25.

31. Ibid., pp. 19, 23; idem, *The Cross of Calvary* (Dorset, England: The Overcomer Literature Trust, n.d.), pp. 35, 37-40, 62-63.

32. Kinnear, *Against the Tide*, p. 50.

33. Watchman Nee, *The Orthodoxy of the Church* (Los Angeles: The Stream Publishers, 1970), pp. 73-74.

34. 1 Corinthians 11:26.

35. Watchman Nee, *Twelve Baskets Full*, 6 vols. (Hong Kong: Hong-Kong Church Book Room, 1966), 2:38-39.

36. Idem, *Spiritual Reality or Obsession* [trans. Stephen Kaung] (New York: Christian Fellowship Publishers, Inc., 1970), passim.

37. Kinnear, *Against the Tide*, p. 73.

38. Lee, *Nee*, pp. 85-88

39. Ibid., p. 203.

40. Lawrence M Tierney and others, eds., *Current Medical Diagnosis & Treatment* (McGraw-Hill, 2000), p. 301.

41. Watchman Nee, *Orthodoxy*, pp. 86-96.

42. Ibid., p. 95.

43. Idem, *The Latent Power of the Soul* [trans. Stephen Kaung] (New York: Christian Fellowship Publishers, Inc., 1972), p.

44. Witness Lee, *The Baptism in the Holy Spirit* (Los Angeles: The Stream Publishers, 1969), p. 12.

45. Nee, *Latent Power*, pp. 48-54; idem, *Spiritual Man*, 1:38-39, 169.

46. Interview with Mrs. Carol Stearns, Church at Hollis, Hollis, New York, October 14, 1972.

47. Kinnear, *Against the Tide*, p. 104.

48. Walter J. Hollenweger, "Unusual Methods of Evangelism in the Pentecostal Movement in China," *A Monthly Letter about Evangelism* nos. 8/9 (November/ December 1965); Stanley H. Frodsham, *With Signs Following* (Springfield, Mo.: Gospel Publishing House, 1946), pp. 121-141.

49. Keswick Convention Trustees, *The Keswick Convention* 1938 (London: Pickering & Inglis Ltd., 1938), p. 245.

50. Watchman Nee, *The Normal Christian Life* (Fort Washington, Penn.: Christian Literature Crusade, 1961), pp. 106-21. On this chapter one scholar has said: "L' éxegése du chapitre´de l'épitre aux Romains a été étudiée é plusieurs reprises, soit é la Convention même, soit dans des livres ou des commentaires écrits dans la ligne de pensée de Keswick." Jean Marc Cruvellier, L'Exégèse de Romains 7 et Le Movemment de Keswick (Amsterdam: Drukkerij Pasmans, 1961), p. 115.

51. Watchman Nee, *The Normal Christian Church Life*, rev. ed. (Washington, D.C.: International Students Press, 1969), p. 99.

52. Ibid., p. 8.

53. Ibid., p. 101.

54. Kinnear, *Against the Tide*, p. 126.

55. Lee, *Nee*, p. 98.

56. Chan, *My Uncle*, pp. 46-50.

57. Nee, *Church Life*, p. 75.

58 Lee, *Nee*, p. 177.

59. Nee, *Church Life*, pp. 50-52.

60. Chan, *My Uncle*, p. 50.

61. Lyall, *Mighty Men*, p. 85.

62. George N. Patterson, *Christianity in Communist China* (Waco, Texas: Word Books, 1969), pp. 38, 72-73, 79-80, 119, 134, 140-41. Mary Wang, *Stephen the Chinese Pastor* (London: Hodder & Stoughton, 1973), p. 98.

63. *Wang, Stephen*, p. 98.

64. Charles E. Notson, "Individualism Gone Astray: The 'Little Flock' of Watchman Ngnee," *The Alliance Weekly*, November 12, 1952, pp. 729-30. David M. Paton, *Christian Missions and the Judgment of God* (London: S.C.M., 1953), p. 49.

65. Notson, "Individualism," p. 730.

66. Paton, *Christian Missions*, p. 49.

67. Miss Helen Willis, quoted by Patterson, *Christianity*, p. 44.

68. Kinnear, *Against the Tide*, p. 154.

69. Cheung, *Ecclesiology*, p. 161.

70. Kinnear, *Against the Tide*, p. 146.

71. Ibid., p. 155.

72. *Tien Feng Magazine*, February 6, 1956, cited by *China Bulletin* 6, no. 6 (March 19, 1956):2.

73. Kinnear, *Against the Tide*, p. 177.

74. Harold G. King, "How I Kept Strong in Faith in a Communist Prison," *The Watchtower*, July 15, 1963, pp. 437-39.

75. Lyall, *Mighty Men*, p. 92.

76. Lee, *Nee*, p. 190.

77. Watchman Nee, *Further Talks on the Church Life* (Taipei: Gospel Book Room, 1968), p. 160.

78. Burton Crane, "Evangelist Drive Sweeps Formosa," *New York Times*, October 8, 1950, p. 11.

79. Hollenweger, *The Pentecostals*, pp. 6-7.

80. Stephen Kaung, *The Song of Degrees* (New York: Christian Fellowship Publishers, 1970), p. 103.

81. Stephen Kaung, *The Splendor of His Ways* (New York: Christian Fellowship Publishers, Inc., 1974), pp. 82- .

82. Ibid., p. 88.

83. Ibid., p. 96.

84. Ibid., pp. 116-18, 126.

85. Cheung, *Ecclesiology*, passim.

86. Ibid., pp. 38,48-50, 85-86.

87. Ibid., pp. 151-73.

88. Lo Shan [Pseud.], "From 'The Case of Fraud in the Church': To See the Conspiracy of the Secret Organization, Part II;" *Nan Pei Chi* 33 (February 16, 1973):44-46.

89. Lee's studies on human nature are contained in his books *The Economy of God* (Los Angeles: The Stream Publishers, 1968) and *The Parts of Man* (Los Angeles: The Stream Publishers, 1969).

90. Witness Lee, "The Indwelling Christ: The Indwelling Christ in Galatians, Part One;" *The Stream* 13:1 (February 1975):3.

91. As he did in *The Economy of God*, p. 82.

92. Idem, *Christ vs. Religion* (Taipei: The Gospel Book Room, [1971]), p. 77.

93. Ibid., p. 101.

94. As described in FF. Bruce, "Interpretation (Biblical)," in *Baker's*

Dictionary of Theology, ed. Everett F. Harrison (Grand Rapids: Baker Book House, 1973), pp. 291-93, and in A. Berkeley Mickelson's book, *Interpreting the Bible* (Grand Rapids: William B. Eerdmans Publishing Company, 1963), passim. In both writers objective concerns provide balance to the subjective concerns of exposition.

95. Lee, *Christ vs. Religion*, pp. 42-43.

96. Heinrich Schlier, "... in *Theological Dictionary of the New Testament*, eds. Kittle, Gerhard and Freidrich, Gerhard 1:180-85 and M.R.W. Fatter, "Heresy," *In Baker's* p. 268.

CHAPTER TWO

Introduction to
Nee's Literature

Watchman Nee's faithfulness to his beliefs in the face of
political hostility and his position as a Chinese church
leader contributed greatly to his significance in the history
of the church. Nevertheless, it is the publication of his Bible
studies that have been most responsible for the popularity
that has occurred subsequent to his public ministry. As of
January 2005, fifty-five volumes have appeared in English,
with an indeterminate amount in preparation.

Of these books, only his three-volume study, *The Spiritual
Man*, was originally written in book form. The rest of the
titles are the result of editing of two other sources: Nee's
magazine articles and the notes of his lectures.

Before 1948, Nee edited four different Christian
magazines: *The Revival* (January 1923-25, 1928-1934), *The
Christian* (1923-1928, 1934-1940), and *The Bible Record* (ca.
1925). In 1948, the old periodicals were replaced by the
new: *The Ministry* (June 1948-?) and The Gospel (1948-).
The earlier *Revival* (translated by Lee as *The Present
Testimony*) was revived until 1951 when all publications
ceased. The format of these periodicals was by and large
modeled after Jessie Penn-Lewis's *The Overcomer* and T.

Austin-Sparks's *A Witness and A Testimony*: (1) an editorial[1]*
by Nee or another co-worker, (2) a long excerpt from the
writings of Andrew Murray, F.B. Meyer, or one of the other
devotional writers he had become familiar with, and (3) a
Bible study prepared from Nee's spoken ministry or, in some
instances, articles written specifically for the magazine.

A preponderance of his material comes from English
and Mandarin shorthand† notes taken during his many lectures
in China and abroad. Some were edited by Nee and printed
in his magazines and booklets, thereby receiving the benefit
of his own authorization. Other texts have only recently been
published into Chinese and a host of other languages. While
these notes provide us with a prolific source of Nee's
theology, the messages are more vulnerable to alterations as
the result of editing.

For example, in *Twelve Baskets Full*, volume three,
chapters ten and eleven are designated by the anonymous
editor as "Selections from *The Normal Christian Life*." But
when we compare this text with that of Kinnear's full text
edition, it is evident that the edited text has been trimmed
down by taking sentences from different paragraphs and
joining them into new cohesive paragraphs. Carefully done,
this form of editing can be an appropriate form of abridgment.
In one instance, the editor does leave in a complete anecdote
by Nee, which provides us with two comparable variations.
(See next page.)

How are these differences to be explained? The reference
to "preaching in the villages of China" could well have been
omitted for purposes of editing. But what caused the "book"/

---

* See Appendix B.

† A less complicated system than the ancient "regular" form of writing,
Mandarin shorthand (Kuan Hua Tzu Mu) contains only 70 characters instead
of the usual 4,000. Miss Elizabeth Fischbacher recorded Nee's messages
in direct translation into English.[3]

Kinnear Text

I remember once I took up a small book and put a piece of paper into it, and I said to those very simple folk [Chinese villagers], "Now look carefully. I take a piece of paper. It has an identity of its own, quite separate from this book. Having no special purpose for it at the moment, I put it into the book. Now I do something with the book. I post it to Shanghai. I do not post the paper, but the paper has been put into the book. Then where is the paper? Can the book go to Shanghai and the paper remain here? Can the paper have a separate destiny from the book? No! Where the book goes the paper goes. If I drop the book in the river the paper goes too, and if I quickly take it out again I recover the paper also. Whatever the experience the book goes through the paper goes through with it, for it is still there in the book."

"Of him are ye in Christ Jesus."[4]

Edited Text

For instance, I put a treasury note in my Bible. Now I mail the Bible to Shanghai. Can the Bible get to Shanghai and the note remain here? No; where the Bible goes the note goes, and whatever the Bible goes through, the note goes through too, for it is in the Bible.

"Of him are ye in Christ Jesus."[5]

"Bible"* and "paper"/ "treasury note" textual variations? These variants are not the result of differences in translation. It seems unlikely that the texts are from two different lectures, since Nee believed that a minister should never repeat his sermons.[6]

Annotated Bibliography

Before systematically examining his epistemology, anthropology, and ecclesiology, it is important first to understand the historical order and direction of the literature from his teaching ministry. All of these works can be chronologically divided into three periods of theological development: the periods from 1923 to 1935, from 1936 to 1942, and from 1946 to 1951.

Spiritual Growth

In the early period, from 1923 to 1935, according to Nee's own testimony, the work was "to assist God's children in their spiritual life and spiritual warfare."[7] Earliest copies of his magazines include his own articles and those of Westerners, such as Jessie Penn-Lewis, who specialized in prayer and spiritual warfare. There is little instruction on the operation of the church but rather Bible studies and instruction on personal spiritual growth and assessing the biblical evidence of God's working in human nature and history. The theology of this period is not original, for it is easily identifiable with Plymouth Brethren and Keswick exegesis.

In *The Spiritual Man*, Nee presents his most thorough interpretation of biblical anthropology. By further distinguishing the functions of the human spirit into intuition, communion, and conscience, and of the soul into emotion, mind and will, Nee feels the believer can properly test

---

* In Mandarin the Bible is Sheng[4]-Shu[1] and book is Shu.[1]

whether religious practices are of God or "soulish" deceptions. This distinguishing between "soulical" and "spiritual" conduct permeates all of his messages on Christian maturity and influences all his theology.

During 1930-1931, Nee prepared a series of fifty questions and answers on Bible doctrines, posthumously published as *Gospel Dialogue*. Grace, sin, justification, sanctification, forgiveness, the atonement, and perfection are defined in a manner similar to Keswick's admixture of Calvinism and perfectionism.

At about the same time, the messages in *Spiritual Reality or Obsession* were given. Containing only sixty-four pages in its present publication format, the work is a prolegomenon to his ideas on the nature of our spiritual knowledge within the church. For the Christian there are only two choices in relation to spiritual truth. He will either be "obsessed"/ deceived into upholding falsehood instead of truth, or he will touch the "reality" of God through the guidance of the Holy Spirit working in the inner man. This working of God in the individual is undertaken by walking in the light of God and is a salient feature of Keswick and Brethren writers who have been influenced by evangelical pietism.[8]

In the summer of 1932, before Nee had any personal contact with Pentecostals, he wrote a series of articles in *Revival Magazine* questioning the origins of tongues, parapsychic phenomena, and the ecstatic practices of other religions. Relying on the conclusions of Mrs. Penn-Lewis's *Soul and Spirit* and G.H. Pember's *Earth's Earliest Ages*, the articles are a sequel to the tripartite theology of *The Spiritual Man* and have been republished collectively in *The Latent Power of the Soul*.

In 1934, Nee gave a Bible study in Hankow, China, in which the Song of Songs was interpreted in terms of spiritual communion. His interpretations (*The Song of Songs*) are a continuation of his concern for the reality of the spiritual life in the church. The material seems to be an integration of Penn-Lewis's commentary, *Thy Hidden Ones,* and Mr. C.A. Coates's *An Outline of the Song of Solomon.* Nee is careful to study the actual content of the text and avoids both the overspiritualization of Mrs. Penn-Lewis and the false "shepherd hypothesis."*

Nee again underlined the need for spiritual reality in a series of messages (*Spiritual Knowledge*) focusing on the way to true self-understanding. This self-understanding is not undertaken by psychoanalytic introspection, but by God revealing the need for our minds to be renewed and our hearts to be circumcised. The method for this transformation of the Christian personality is God's working in the inner man as understood in Nee's trichotomous anthropology.

Come, Lord Jesus is a study of the Book of Revelation. In his preface, Stephen Kaung, the translator and editor, explains that his original mimeograph notes on Rev. 2:19-3:22 were missing. To provide a continuous running commentary, portions of *The Orthodoxy of the Church* were substituted. *God's Plan and the Overcomers,* written in 1934, explains how a portion of God's people will ultimately play an important part in the millennium and Christ's second coming. These two works provide much of the material used in interpreting his eschatology. See Chapter 5, "The Church in the Eschaton."

The Antioch Principle
By the summer of 1937, the Japanese had begun their World War II drive into the heartland of China. With a large migration of refugees and the opportunity open to evangelize in other parts of the country, Nee realized the necessity of establishing

---

* In this interpretation, there are three principle characters in The Song of Solomon: Solomon, the Shulamite maiden, and her shepherd lover.[9]

some form of guidelines for the structure and missionary work of his local church. The church must now be instructed in the truths contained in the Corinthian

Epistles (polity), as Nee saw it, in addition to the Word from the Ephesian Epistle (sanctification). Consecration and church vocational guidance are also important parts of this teaching period. Within the next three and a half years, ten volumes were produced, representing his most popular and probably his most original material.

Before this, any one of the churches established by Watchman Nee could accurately be described as a lay sect established on Brethren principles of opposition to professional clergy, to extralocal authority, to denominationalism, and to formal membership, with an additional emphasis on the spiritual life of the individual. A change came as a result of the teachings offered in *The Normal Christian Church Life* (original title: *Rethinking Our Missions*). After examining the activities of his own work and the evidence of Scripture, Nee suggested guidelines of church order for his mission-oriented churches. Apostles were missionaries, who by the charism administered by God and by the recognition of the church, served in the sphere of the church universal. The elders were the leaders of the church local. Since the church at Antioch in the Book of Acts was the most missionary-conscious of the New Testament churches, it should be the model of the Chinese Church. Furthermore, since no city or town is described as having two congregations, there must be one church for one locality.

His unique emphasis on the "ground of locality" created no controversy among the members of the Little Flock churches.* As a minority movement in a minority religion, Nee's churches were still too small and economically weak

---

[37] From here on, Nee's assemblies shall be called the local churches.

to have more than one church in one location. The movement's singleness of purpose (building up God's church in love) prevented the congregations from developing any schismatic diversity. Even after Nee's local church movement had become a divided sect, "locality" became the doctrine and pattern of the mission work. Any church formed apart from these principles was considered to be in error. Even in the book *The Normal Christian Church Life*, which Mo-Oi Cheung regarded as the written expression of Nee's church local, what matters most are not ecclesiastical methods, but the nature of man:

> ... what matters most is the man, not his methods. Unless the man is right, right methods will be of no use to him or his work. Carnal methods are suited to carnal men, and spiritual methods to spiritual men. For carnal men to employ spiritual methods will only result in confusion and failure.[10]

Two books came out of his trip to Europe the following year. *The Normal Christian Life* describes the progress of the believer towards the goal of absolute surrender to God according to Romans 5-8. The publishers introduce the work as "a spiritual classic,"[11] and indeed the American edition has already sold well over 600,000 copies. The central theme is one of a progressive Godward "abiding in Him," yet as is characteristic of Nee's exegesis, chapter seven dwells at length upon God's response to the spirit and the soul.

Sit, Walk, Stand has much of this same emphasis on spiritual growth. Here Nee summarizes the message of Ephesians, according to Paul's distinctive use of verbs,* relative to the soteriological disposition of the believer. Speaking to Holiness groups in England and Europe, these

---

* The three verbs are in 1:20, 2:6 (Kathizö/sugkathizö); 4:1, 17; 5:2, 8 (peripateö); and 6:11, 13, 14 (histemi).

messages were heard by receptive ears. His theology is totally that of the Keswick teaching, with a gracious and illustrative style equal to that of Andrew Murray and F.B. Meyer.

A series of addresses on the Christian's attitude toward the world given from 1938 to 1941, together with a few adjunctive sermons, comprise the book *Love Not the World*. Enroth, Ericson, and Peters, in their study of the Jesus People, have unduly criticized this book for its "anti-cultural fundamentalism."[12] Nee makes no apologies for his disappointment that the earth's resources have fallen into "unconsecrated hands."[13] The solution is not the world-abandoning escapism of such premillennial cults as the Children of God, but:

> … today the church has a definite responsibility before God to register the victory of Christ in the Devil's territory. If there is to be a testimony to the principalities and powers, if the impact of Christ's sovereignty through His Cross is to be registered in the spiritual realm, it can only be as the judicial foothold in our hearts of the "pretender" in the race is met, and by the same Cross, removed and repudiated. For God's object is still that man should "have dominion." Our work for Him does not stop with proclaiming a Gospel that was designed merely to undo the effect of Genesis 3, marvelous as was that undoing. God wants also to take us back further to Genesis 1 itself.[14]

Nee continues by saying that the purification of the world is coincident with the consecration of the spirit: "Godward that in itself effectually deprives Satan of any moral ground in us he may claim to possess."[15]

Another important theme arising out of Nee's messages is recognizing God's call for service—illustratively expressed in *What Shall This Man Do?*. There are only three emphases of ministry in the New Testament. Whether God calls a worker to minister in the style of Peter (the proclaimer of salvation who serves as the fisher of men), Paul (the tentmaker, the builder of God's house) or John (as a mender of nets, he restores the churches) depends upon the will of God preparing him even before the believer's renaissance. For Paul says, "Let each man abide in that calling wherein he was called."[16] And for Nee, this abiding comes about as we are open to the Lord's many opportunities to enlarge our ministry. It is more a question of letting God activate us in His body than our determining our ministry's course and function.

Beginning at the end of the year 1939, Nee gave five lectures on Christ and His relationship to the believer. As its English title suggests (*Christ The Sum of All Spiritual Things*), a high Christology is proposed:

> One day I was talking to a group of people about this spiritual fact. As I spoke, many eyes stared at me. I told them I would present a most significant fact to them; namely, that God's Christ is God's everything, for God has nothing else but Christ! God has not given us light, He gives Christ to us; God has not given us food, He gives Christ to us; God has not given us the way, the truth, and the life, instead He gives us Christ. God's Christ is all things; aside from Him, God has nothing.[17]

Such ontological abstractions here may be one source for Witness Lee's modalism.[18] Here at least Nee is orthodox enough to understand that Christ is all things in that He is the subject and sum of all our needs. God has not given us many things outside of Christ. Therefore, prayers offered for healing, patience, and other works of grace must be directed to the fulfillment of Christ's resurrection life in our whole being.

The homiletical style of Nee's teachings is quite evident in *Changed into His Likeness*.[19] Why is it that God tells Moses at Sinai that He is "the God of Abraham, the God of Isaac, and the God of Jacob" (Exodus 3:6)? The question actuates

Nee's talents into formulating a sermon in the common three-point form. Guided by Romans 9-11 and Galatians 3ff., Nee thought this triple refrain must together represent the spiritual experience of all God's people.

Abraham was chosen by God in His sovereign grace apart from any righteousness—because Abraham was a worshiper of idols when God called him—and apart from any physical effort. For us, Abraham represents our hope of reaching the final promised land.

Isaac typifies Christ in that he embodies God's plan and willingly accepts his place in God's sacrificial system, "passively." Isaac provides the transition between Abraham's life of promise and Jacob's life, which signals the transformation of human nature through Christ.

These analogies are a bit farfetched, particularly when he sees two works of grace in the believer through Jacob's experiences at Peniel and El-bethel. Throughout this homily, the contrast between the spiritual man and the natural man embodies the essential hindrance in our striving to be formed into God's likeness.

Perhaps correctly understanding wartime needs, in *God's Work*[20] Nee prepared other Christians to better comprehend the mystery of their responsibility in God's redemptive plan. For the church to survive the coming occupation, it had to do more than save souls. Outwardly the church has a clear mission and command to preach the gospel, but inwardly it needs the revelation of God's will to further build up the body of Christ in order to overcome the sicknesses of this world. For without God revealing His will in the hearts of the one ministering and the one ministered to, the church's work will be ineffectual and vacant of spiritual life. Therefore, Nee believed, the church must "deeply know the cross, . . . know the cross within and bear it daily."[21] In a sense, once the body surrenders itself to the redemption of the cross, it will receive resurrection power—ever-revealing God's will for His people. "We refuse all service," Nee says, "which is only to man."[22] For as priests our service is also Godward and needs to first go through the death of the cross, which will purify us and crucify "the natural life." Once undertaken "the Lord gives us grace to enter into the Holy of Holies because all of self and all of man and all of mixture and all of earth has been destroyed in death but what is indestructible and what is deathless has emerged in resurrection life."[23] Here again Nee supports his argument with an anthropological theme: redemption through the cross working in human nature.

Shortly before the fall of Shanghai, he preached a series of five messages on prayer. Quite consistently, he begins his thesis with a talk on man's divinely pronounced authority of free will. For this reason man has a unique place and purpose in Nee's theology. Man is the only aspect of creation that can restrict the divine purpose. In God's design, Nee believes, man has been given a conscious choice between being one with, or divided from, His eternal will. In the Christian life the former is implemented through the medium of prayer— honoring God's name, inaugurating God's kingdom upon the earth, and thus invoking God's will. This study was later published in the United States under the title, *The Prayer Ministry of the Church.*[24]

The Jerusalem Principle

We may mark the third and final literary period with the war's end in 1945 and Nee's final resignation from the pharmaceutical firm. Shortly thereafter Nee gave an exposition on the seven churches in the Book of Revelation. His thoughts on Ephesus, Smyrna, Pergamum, Thyatira, and Sardis are not very original, reflecting the historical dispensational approach, where each church is representative of God's judgment upon periods of church history.[25] With the exception of Smyrna, these church ages had lost sight of the apostolic vision of the church of Jesus Christ. It is not until the advent of the Philadelphia church that the people of God "recover" the apostolic tradition.

Specifically, this new, wholly reformed church began in 1825 with the Plymouth Brethren. In the published text of this Bible study, the presumed return to ecclesiastical orthodoxy included denominational and clerical iconoclasm:

> These believers, in the world's eye, were lowly and unknown. But they had the Lord in their midst and the consolation of the Holy Spirit. They stood on the ground of two clear truths: firstly, that the church is the Body of Jesus Christ and that this Body is only one; secondly, in the New Testament there is no clergy system; all the ministers of the Word set up by men are not scriptural. They believed that all true believers are the members of this one Body.[26]

These two principles are extolled in many of his books and were the guiding principles of the Little Flock. Yet, Nee warned both the local churches and the Brethren of the ever-present danger of becoming lukewarm in their faithful and true witness, as did the church of Laodicea. The only preventive against this was for each member of every congregation to be an "overcomer." As chapter four will explain, he defines this overcoming state by means of an anthropological soul/spirit dialectic.

Two years later, Nee gave a talk to fellow workers in Foochow on the sanctifying work of the cross through the breaking of the outward man (the soul/body) to allow the release of the spirit. The published version, *The Release of the Spirit*, has become exceedingly popular for its description of the somatic/psychic/pneumatic dynamics of the spiritual life.

In February of 1948, the "Jerusalem principle" geographically focused Nee's teaching ministry almost entirely within the city of Foochow. A total of nine books have been published from the work there.

While *The Normal Christian Church Life* presents the theoretical and political framework of Nee's concept of the church, his Basic Lesson Series[27] contains the outline and guidelines of the practical church life. His teachings on deliverance (Romans 7), prayer, praise, thanksgiving, the simple life, the sacraments, sex and marriage, evangelism, and the conduct of worship are further explained through exposition of pertinent passages. Much of the material presented in earlier writings is summarized, and it can be said with some justification that the six volumes of the series represent a collation of his practical theology. As such, Nee avoids the anthropological emphasis of his earlier works. He provides in the fourth volume:

> During the past twenty years, I have received enough letters and met enough people to certify how often Christians try to examine their inner feelings. After they are told of the separation of spirit and soul, they start to analyze themselves day in and day out. They inwardly become a laboratory where they unceasingly analyze what is right and what is not right. This is most unhealthy and is a symptom of sickness. We should not allow God's children to do that.[28]

Such cautions had been a concern with Nee since the beginning of his ministry.[29] Yet, he continued to write on the subject for those capable of deriving help from such teaching. For example, *Ye Search the Scriptures*, which chronologically follows the Basic Lesson Series, is a book that deals just as much with Christian anthropology as it does with Bible study. Over half of the text discusses the preparation of the man best able to use his proposed Bible study methods. Again in *The Ministry of God's Word*, the intent of the book is not so much to teach homiletic techniques, but to reveal to the preacher and teacher that his flesh "must be transformed according to the requirements of God's Word."[30]

Quite important to the local churches under the new "Jerusalem principle" of church organization is the question of authority.[31] In *Spiritual Authority* Nee declares that all authority comes from God. Those who rebel against authority are full of human thought and reason, and God's rule in their life is blocked. While we must submit to all authority, we are not commanded to obey those authorities who clearly command contrary to the will of God (Scripture). Instruction is given in spiritual discernment between God-delegated authority and ungodly rule.

The last book coming out of the Foochow teaching center is *The Normal Christian Worker*. Like many of his other writings, a practical set of guidelines is not his purpose, but the spiritual advance of the worker's inner life. The necessary implements of service, diligence, stability, love, honesty, and long-suffering are there for the worker who wishes to be free from the soulish activity and whose heart, mind and spirit are open to God's purposes.[32]

Further Talks on the Church Life is a collection of essays given in the later years of Nee's public ministry. Chapter six is the oldest essay and was given in August 1948. It contains a representation of the Jerusalem principle. The rest of the chapters are but amplifications of his ecclesiology of locality. Written after the fall of China, when church leadership seemed threatened, the themes of unity and preserving local church polity dominate the content of these, his public, messages.

Practical Issues of This Life, The Glory of His Life and *The Body of Christ: A Reality* are three collections of essays given at various times and then edited according to certain general themes. Theologically they offer little in the way of insights into the governing principles of Nee's teachings. As the first title suggests, they are examples of Nee's practical applications of the instruction given in such works as *The Normal Christian Life, The Spiritual Man,* and *The Normal Christian Church Life.*

Two anthologies have been published. *A Table in the Wilderness* contains daily meditations from his writings. *Twelve Baskets Full* is a four-volume series containing "fragments" from his entire Christian life.

The work of translation and publication continues, and it is reasonable to assume that the present list of works will be expanded to include a sizable number of future publications. While there is still much of Nee's career unaccounted for by the present publications, there is sufficient evidence from Kinnear's biography and Witness Lee's account to be confident that the fundamentals of Nee's theology are already present in the books just described.

Style

Any reader of Watchman Nee's writings is conscious of a pervasive devotional style in all but one of his works.* From the beginning, Nee emphasized that his work, as is all of the church's work, is to be dominated by the "spiritual." By this Nee meant that the church must be concerned with allowing the human spirit to touch the spiritual reality, which is the church's revelation from God. All must be spiritual. "Whatever may be entered into without the guidance of the Holy Spirit," Nee says, "is definitely not spiritual reality."[33] The church achieves this reality by developing and nurturing, not the carnal man, but the spiritual man. This is the sum and substance of the literature of Watchman Nee.

---

* Only in *Come, Lord Jesus* (New York: Christian Fellowship Publishers, 1976) does the text resemble an interpretive exegesis of a biblical text.

Chapter 2 Endnotes

1. C.T. Chan's memoir contains a number of these editorials, particularly during the period between 1928-33. *My Uncle*, pp. 16-17, 20-24, 74-129.

2. D.S. Murray, "The Church in Village Communities: I. Twenty Years Experience in Northern China," *International Review of Missions* 7 (1918):371.

3. Angus Kinnear to Dana Roberts, April 17, 1975, personal letter.

4. Nee, *Christian Life*, pp. 31-32.

5. Nee, *Twelve Baskets* 2:83-84.

6. Nee, *The Ministry*, pp. 134-35.

7. Nee, *Testimony*, p. 16.

8. F. Ernest Stoeffler's *The Rise of Evangelical Pietism* (Leiden: E.J. Brill, 1965) clearly shows that pietism was a strong influence upon the minds of evangelical leaders in England during the eighteenth and nineteenth century. The Keswick "Higher Life" Movement and Brethren groups were further influenced by their association with continental pietists: Keswick, through its close kinship with German Gemeinschaftsbewegung (Fellowship Movement); Brethrenism, through J.N. Darby's association with French pietism and George Miiller's reading of the works of German Pietist August Hermann Francke (1663-1727). Donald Bloesch, *The Evangelical Renaissance* (Grand Rapids: William B. Eerdmans Publishing Company, 1973), p. 104; F. Roy Coad, *History of the Brethren Movement* (Grand Rapids: William B. Eerdmans Publishing Company, 1968), pp. 45, 48; B.B. Warfield, *Perfectionism*, ed. Samuel G. Craig (Philadelphia: Presbyterian and Reformed Publishing Company, 1971), pp. 312-48.

9. H.H. Rowley, "The Interpretation of the Song of Songs," *Journal of Theological Studies* 38 (1937): 350-51.

10. Nee, *Church Life*, p. 12.

11. Idem, *Christian Life*, back cover.

12. Enroth, Ericson and Peters, *The Jesus People*, p. 169.

13. Nee, *Love Not the World*, (Fort Washington, Pa.: Christian Literature Crusade, 1968), p. 14.

14. Ibid., p. 85.

15. Ibid., p. 86.

16. 1 Corinthians 7:20.

17. Watchman Nee, *Christ the Sum of All Spiritual Things*, [trans. Stephen Kaung] (New York: Christian Fellowship Publishers, Inc., 1973), p. 59.

18. Witness Lee, *The Economy of God*, pp. 10-11. Alan Wallerstedt, Spiritual Counterfeits Project, personal letter.

19. Watchman Nee, *Changed into His Likeness* (Fort Washington, Pa.: Christian Literature Crusade, 1967).

20. Idem, *God's Work* (New York: Christian Fellowship Publishers, Inc., 1974). The book was produced from Miss Fischbacher's notes of a seminar given between June 11 and June 18, 1940.

21. Ibid., p. 27.

22. Ibid., p. 55.

23. Ibid.

24. Idem, *The Prayer Ministry of the Church* (New York: Christian Fellowship Publishers, Inc., 1973).

25. As found in C.I. *Scofield's Reference Bible* (New York: Oxford University Press, 1909), pp. 1332-34.

26. Nee, *Orthodoxy*, p. 69.

27. The series is published by Christian Fellowship Publishers (New York) and includes *A Living Sacrifice* (1972), *The Good Confession* (1973), *Assembling Together* (1973), *Not I but Christ* (1974), *Do All to the Glory of God* (1974) and *Love One Another* (1975).

28. Nee, *Not I, But Christ*, p. 135.

29. Idem, *Spiritual Man*, 1:17 ff.

30. Idem, *The Ministry of God's Word* (New York: Christian Fellowship Publishers, 1971), p. 15.

31. See pp. 148 ff.

32. See idem, *The Normal Christian Worker* (Hong Kong: Hong Kong Church Book Room, 1965), pp. 16, 133.

33. Nee, *Spiritual Reality*, p. 6.

The Word and Its Ministry

At the forefront of all Christian theology, there is one central issue: How do we know God through His Word? Watchman Nee and his movement challenged and broke with much of what in the mission community he considered to be the traditions of men. As Karl Barth reacted to the weaknesses in German liberalism, so also Nee objected to the denominational strife and theological divisions among the different missionary societies. Nee and Barth's responses were in part a reaffirmation of the church's epistemological roots in the Word of God. But while Barth unhesitatingly drew a wedge between the inerrant Word of God and the human witness of that Word in Scripture and preaching,[1] Nee sees the scriptural witnesses as inerrant through the sanctifying activity of the Holy Spirit in the spiritual man.

The Word

Nee does not specify the Word of God in a threefold form as Barth does,[2] but rather describes the Word in terms of the various ministrations found in three kinds of people. In the Old Testament, the Word came to the prophets in a way that did not "mingle" with their own opinions, feelings, or thoughts. God only used their voices and controlled them to the extent that the Word might not be tainted by human error. But there were Moses, Isaiah, David, and Jeremiah, whose personal feelings mirrored those of God enough that they could use them to speak the Word of God. While they acted mostly under an Old Testament prophetic form, their ministry foreshadowed New Testament apostolic principles.[3]

In Jesus, the Word becomes flesh. Not only His voice but also His thoughts, feelings and opinion communicated the Word. No longer is the Word objectively presented to the house of Israel alone, but it is also presented subjectively to all men. It is God's desire that His Word should carry human feelings, thoughts, and ideas through the personality of Jesus. Nee implies that the Old Testament office of prophet finds its completion in Jesus. For, "When He opened His mouth there was God's Word; even when He shut His mouth, God's Word was still there, for as a Person He is the Word of God."[4]

In Jesus, the Word is fully consistent with the flesh. In the New Testament ministry of the apostles, therefore, the flesh must be transformed according to God's Word in order that the flesh might become the instrument to communicate that Word in a divine and human form. This is the basis of the Word in the writers of the New Testament and of every Christian minister of the Word.

Nee therefore does not believe, as Barth does,[5] that the preaching of God's Word (the ministry) need be contaminated by the human element. Rather it is God's intention that the Word should be subjective by its mingling with the person who is open and obedient to God. While Barth and the neo-orthodox theologians view God's sovereignty as working in human history alone, Nee sees God working sovereignly in the inner man preparing the way of revelation, also.

In every book by Watchman Nee, there is no question that he holds to the central evangelical premise: The Bible is the inspired Word of God. Unlike Barth's teachings, the Bible is not in a state of becoming,[6] for it is already the Word of God. "It reveals to us," Nee says, "all that God has done for us in the past."[7] Now, it is the church's guide to lead us to God and our life in Christ.

The Word Studied

Since it is extremely rare, according to Nee, for God to speak with words not found in the Bible, Nee was concerned to "equip the saints" with the means of effectually studying the Scripture. Instruction in this area does not begin with methods and exegesis, Nee argues; the man himself must be primary:

> Consequently, in approaching this matter of searching the Scriptures, we should naturally divide it into two parts: first, the preparation of man; second, the methods of Bible study.[8]

Quoting the words of Jesus in John 6:63, Nee begins his study of the human preparation by stating that the words of the Bible are more than words, "they are also spirit."[9] It is not the unregenerate, "natural man" who can understand the meaning of the Bible. It is not for the carnal believer who has the Spirit without submitting to God's authority (his understanding of the Bible is quite limited). But it is the spiritual man who is taught in God's wisdom by the Holy Spirit, "combining spiritual things with spiritual words."[10]* He knows that the Bible is without error or contradiction. He has the Spirit's interpretation and is personally cognitive of the inner Word of God, outwardly expressed in the words of the Bible.†

---

* Nee also comments on the American Standard Version, marginal translation, "interpreting spiritual things to spiritual men." Nee's thoughts here are derived in large part from his interpretation of 1 Corinthians 2-3.
† "The distinctiveness of this Book is its dual feature: on the one hand the Bible has its outer shell—the physical part of the Bible—similar to the part of man which is made of dust; on the other hand it has its spiritual part, that which is in the Holy Spirit, what is God breathed and God spoken."[11]

This is a cardinal point in understanding the style and character of the writings of Watchman Nee, and helps to explain some of the eccentric tendencies among members of the small flock churches. By their hermeneutics-of-the-spiritual-man principle, Nee and his followers are quick to reject all forms of liberalism and higher criticism. Nee writes:

> If a person is not regenerated, then no matter how clever and scholarly he may be, to him this book is a mystery. But a regenerated man whose cultural background may be quite primitive possesses greater understanding of the Bible than does an unregenerate college professor. And the explanation? One of them has a regenerate spirit, while the other has not. The Scriptures cannot be mastered through cleverness, research, or natural talent. The Word of God is spirit, therefore it can only be known to whoever possesses a regenerated spirit. Since the root and nature of the Bible are spiritual, how can anyone who lacks a regenerated spirit begin to understand it? It is a closed book to him.[12]

Conservative Christianity also comes under such criticism. Much of the theological divisions among

Christian churches and missions Nee attributes to individual and therefore private interpretation contrary to 2 Peter 1:20.[13]

It is not enough to have a regenerate spirit. "Man needs not only to possess this spirit," Nee says, "but needs also to be possessed by this spirit."[14] The Spirit must also exercise his spirit, his "god-consciousness," and he must consecrate himself absolutely and entirely to the Lord. While there may be much truth in what Nee says here, the sense of his words was altered in many of the local churches as a result of the leadership vacuum created by Watchman Nee's imprisonment.

Even those writers whom Nee regarded as spiritual* and those who would probably fit his criteria are now regarded by many of the local churches' members as not spiritual enough. They reason that it is a better use of one's time to read only the Bible and Bible interpreters equal to Nee's books in spiritual content. Who is equal to Nee? Among the local church groups that follow this teaching, there are only two modern writers capable of writing on this spiritual plane: Watchman Nee himself and Witness Lee.

In *Ye Search the Scriptures*, a number of methods of Bible study are discussed in detail. These methods and his spiritual criticism of the Bible are not very original, but are quite similar to the Keswick devotional emphasis on Bible study. One need only compare the contents of A.T. Pierson's *The Bible and Spiritual Criticism* with Nee's book. Like Nee, he also believed in the "necessity of the 'Spiritual Man' to perceive, discern, and apprehend the spiritual element in the book [the Bible]."[15]

With these proper methods, in conjunction with the regenerated human spirit, the minister enters or "penetrates" into the things of the Holy Spirit in three ways.[16] First, he enters into the thought or explanation within the Bible and perceives its real meaning. Secondly, he enters into the factual impression of the Holy Spirit presented in each historical incident of the Bible as it relates to the whole working of God. Finally, he enters into the spirit of the Bible. In the Bible, the Holy Spirit has manifested His own feelings through the writers' human spirits. He who is spiritual enters in and "touches" that same Spirit and experiences these same

---

* Among those Bible expositors Nee recommends are Henry Alford, Thomas Chalmers, J.N. Darby, Charles Finney, Jessie Penn-Lewis, Dwight L. Moody, C.H. Mackintosh, Phillip Schaff, William Smith, Hudson Taylor, R.A. Torrey, S.P. Tregelles, B.F. Westcott, and Christopher Wordsworth.

feelings. But without the initial preparation of man, all study of the Bible is without life and is a dead work.

The Minister Sanctified

For Nee the Bible teaches that some men are called to be teaching-elders in the local congregation.[17] They alone are not what Nee means by the ministers of the Word; they only train people to be more effective ministers. All believers have the potential to minister in presenting the Word of God to other people. "A minister of the Word is one who has the revelation of Christ, one in whom God has been pleased to reveal His Son (see Gal. 1:16)."[18] That is, man must first by faith be brought by God to Christ for the knowledge of the Son. Without this "basic revelation," man cannot begin to know the Bible as the Word of God, nor can he impart the Word to others. This knowledge through revelation of the Son Nee describes as a "touch." Like the woman with the issue of blood in Mark 5, it is not enough for man to press around Jesus, he must touch Him "with conscious faith":

> The words which the Lord utters are spirit and life. If you touch this, you touch the ministry of the word. The task is not simply presenting a book to men, rather it is presenting the Son of God in the Book. When a minister of the word serves people with God's Word, he simultaneously serves with the Son of God. We minister with Christ.[19]

Many in the Church, Nee complains, have crowded around the Bible, but have not touched its reality and the Christ within.

The basic revelation is essential to the apostolic post-ascension[20]* ministry, for the Word of God is both the

---

* "The Christian era began with Christ, of whom we are told that, when He had made purification of sins, He 'sat down on the right hand of the Majesty on high' (Hebrews 1:3). With equal truth we can say that the individual Christian life begins with a man 'in Christ'—that is to say, when by faith we see ourselves seated together with Him in the heavens."[20]

incarnate Son of God and the printed Scriptures. The church's present ministry of the Word therefore is founded on its knowledge of Christ and its familiarity with the Bible. For this reason Nee further delimits the minister of the Word to the "one who translates Christ into the Bible; that is, he tells people of the Christ he knows in the words of the Bible so that in those who receive the Bible the Holy Spirit will translate it back into Christ."[21]

How can one receive the basic revelation? Certainly Nee means here nothing less than conversion/regeneration itself.[22] The unrepentant is unable to hear the spiritual Word of God, even though the revelation be present in sight and sound. As a result of the fall his spirit is dead. The penitent who wills to accept the good news by faith is saved.[23] His spirit is quickened, and he sees that Jesus is Lord and surrenders himself. Later he familiarizes himself with the Bible and understands the full meaning of that single, basic revelation.

Nee formulates a second kind of revelation in the life of the minister of God's Word, the detailed revelation. Whereas the first kind (basic) is once for all at our rebirth, the second (detailed) is given time and again. In fact, every occasion wherein the Word is to be ministered must also be the occasion for a fresh revelation according to God's past revelations. For just as the New Testament is based upon the Old Testament revelation, so also the continuing revelation to the church is based on the Scripture and the initial revelation of Jesus as Lord. In a sense Nee appears to see the first revelation as God's gracious Word for the unbeliever, the second as His gracious Word in and through the believer.

Nee depicts revelation as coming to the believer as light.[24] Whether it comes to us in our drawing near to Jesus in prayer, through the ministry of others, or indirectly in studying the Bible diligently, the light swiftly passes.[25] Light easily fades away from our memory. The greater the light to us, the more difficult it is for us to remember. "Many brothers," Nee says, "confess that it is extremely difficult to remember the things they have read of spiritual revelation."[26] The light of revelation shines into the human heart, but God intends it to reach our human understanding (the mind).[27] Indeed this is, as Nee sees it, the problem with tongues without interpretation in 1 Corinthians 14:28 While tongues may be a valid expression of the onset of the divine light, Nee interprets verse 19 as requiring understanding for the ministry (or instructing) of the revelation to others. Nee goes on to describe the role of thought and understanding as one of "fixing" or "anchoring" the light. Without our understanding, we can neither know its content nor claim the revelation in our spirit as ours.

In the Old Testament ministry, it was not necessary for God to use the mind or understanding. Now with the full revelation of Christ's victory over death and His ascension as its antecedents; the New Testament ministry must also minister the same victory and power over the flesh, by God dealing with us.[29] In the language and style of Nee, "the outward man needs to be broken."[30] In brokenness, God examines us and gives us knowledge of our human weaknesses. When God begins to deal with these weaknesses by His power, the broken man becomes rich in His thoughts. In Nee's study on ministry, *The Ministry of God's Word*, there is no single issue more important to him than brokenness. When the outward man is broken, all man's understanding and thought become subservient to whatever light is received by the spirit, and he lives as a spiritual man.

The divine, detailed revelation and the subsequent human, inner thought are not in themselves the message. But they are the essential components of what Nee identifies with the Old Testament prophet's usage of the term *massa*.[31] As the word denotes, revelation and thought become a psychokinetic weight upon the spiritual man. In order to discharge his burden, the minister must seek for the "inner words" or word from God to give oral content to what is as yet inexpressible or ecstatic.

Further defined, the word within is in summary the divinely chosen message for a specific gospel presentation. Strictly conforming to the content of Scripture, it may come as a single word or as many as ten or so sentences. This word, for example, may be, "For by grace have ye been saved through faith" (Eph. 2:8). Here it comes as a complete theological statement, but the listener is left with too many unanswered questions: Why has God reminded us of this now? What is the relationship between faith and grace? Is the emphasis of the minister's burden upon "grace," "faith," or "saved"? For according to Nee, the content is too strong and concentrated to be fully understood and digested by the listener.[32]

The inner word given by the Holy Spirit must now be translated or expanded into the "outer words" of human understanding and experience. This transaction of the divine word is contingent upon the minister's own experience in Christian discipleship. If the minister's experience includes the breaking of the outward man, his words will be spiritual, accurate, of high quality, and "touching" God. Without this experience he is unfit to preach, and his message, while outwardly clever and persuasive, is inwardly immature and unspiritual. The Apostle Paul represents the ideal example. For in 1 Corinthians 7 he speaks without special revelation, yet, he speaks God's Word.[33] For with Paul, as with the contemporary spiritual man, the outer words are created through brokenness in discipline and chastisement, not through purely human abilities. In the continual breaking of the outward man unto perfection, the minister is most successful in distilling the ABCs of saving faith according to the needs and problems of the church and its witness to the world.

The Word Ministered

Nee describes two additional aspects that come into play as the outward word is being presented: memory and feelings.

Some of us by nature have good memories, and Nee believes such abilities can be a real advantage in recalling the inner word. Yet this outward memory too often fails or alters the word as it is delivered. God provides for the mnemonically weak a "Holy Spirit memory"[34] that recalls the spirit or pictures the inner words of revelation.

In the ministry, right feelings must accompany the right words. In order for feelings, "the most delicate part in us,"[35] to be proper, Nee also sees the need for the outward man to be broken. If it is broken, the minister has only the strength of the inner man to rely on.

Trained to speak God's Word, the minister must be willing to minister. He must, as Nee says, be willing to "push your spirit out, else the word will suffer greatly."[36] By this metaphysical push, the spirit is exercised and pours forth from life. While the experience may be quite exhausting,[37] this release of the spirit in ministry is a release of God's power, life, and light to others.

Nee concludes his study of the ministry by offering some helps to speaking and a brief discussion of the audience of the Word.[38] His helps contain no suggestions on homiletical style or technique, for Nee considers such instruction as an encouragement towards preaching by the soul and an assault on the primacy of the spirit. Rather he is concerned to "keep the spirit from being wounded,"[39] through contact with sin(s) or any imperfections of the incarnational dynamics of the word encountered by the minister. In the closing chapter, entitled "The Objects of the Word," Nee concedes that the congregation must also be spiritually attuned to receive spiritual things and can affect the delivery of the word. To the wise and intelligent (Matt. 11:25; 1 Corinthians 1:19), the hardhearted (Matt. 13:15) and those who blaspheme the Holy Spirit, "God is unwilling to reveal himself, therefore He hides from them."[40] Under these circumstances, the minister is hindered in his effort to release the Spirit, and his words suffer.

An essential feature in Nee's theology of the Word is his inflexible belief that God has not failed in the performance of His will. Part of that will is God's wish to use man:

> Man was created for God's specific purpose. As He did not make an obedient machine at the time of creation, so He now rejects the use of a preaching machine. He does not want an automaton; He wants a man with free will. It is a calculated risk with God to choose man as a minister of His word. Yet in spite of the complexity of man and his many problems such as sin, defilement, weakness, the outward man, and natural resistance, God still entrusts His word to man. Through the greatest rigor God obtains His highest glory.[41]

In that "calculated risk," both perfect love and man's natural potential to abrogate and eclipse the truth with himself become salient features of biblical and church history. And Watchman Nee understands his service to God in that history is to instruct in the way of the spiritual man, who administers truth.

Nee therefore places great emphasis on understanding the way in which the Holy Spirit overcomes the fallen nature to perfectly reveal the truth. This overcoming process of the Christian to permit perfect revelation in the church is summarized in the illustration and the following page.

While the church has no control over the content of God's sovereign revelation, it is responsible for the presentation and delivery of the message in its individual dealing with the outward man. In his own anthropological style, Nee offers the instruction that the clear revelation enters into the life of the community through the spiritual man.

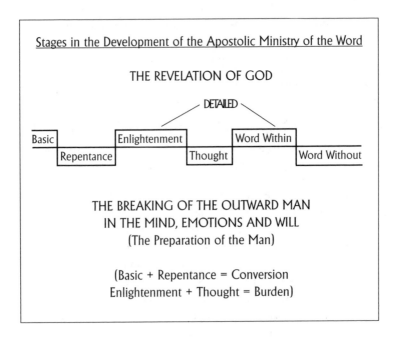

While there may be much truth in Nee's statements that dedicated Christians (spiritual men) are better able to minister the Word of God than a scholarly elite,* Nee and his followers are always precariously close to a Gnostic idea of the church. In such a church setting, membership is not based on salvation in the person of Christ alone, but on the knowledge of spiritual realities. Witness Lee himself has condemned Christendom for not accepting all of Nee's and Lee's "recovered" truths.[42]

Can an unbeliever understand the Bible? Nee says no. But the Bible says yes, but not all can. Psalm 19:7 says, "The commandment of the Lord is clear, enlightening the eyes." You don't have to have or find someone enlightened. The Bible does the enlightening. Psalm 119:130 also says, "The

---

* At least that is one way of interpreting the current rise of the evangelical church. They are better able to communicate to the mind and the needs of the laymen.

unfolding of your words gives light; it imparts understanding to the simple." The simple can understand it. Whether Jesus is teaching great crowds or his disciples, it is easy to see why the Scripture is both impenetrable and simple enough to understand. Jesus keeps asking, "Have you not read ..." (Matt. 12:3, 5;19: 14;22: 31)," Have you never read in the scriptures ..." (Matt. 12:3, 5; 9:13; 12:7; 15:3; 19:14; 21:13, 42; 22:29, 31; John 3:10).[43]

The Gospels tell us and the epistles confirm the fact that it is our devotion to sin that obscures the meaning. The Holy Spirit opens the eyes with those who seek after him. These seekers are "poor in spirit." They know they are not spiritual. Seekers are easy to find. They seek after God because they want to love Him. Seekers are lovers. They understand the love letters of God's Holy Book.

This does not mean that we can understand everything. Even Peter said of Paul's letters, "His letters contain some things that are hard to understand, which ignorant and unstable people distort, as they do the other Scriptures, to their own destruction." (2 Peter 3:16). Yet, Paul tells us in 2 Corinthians 1:13 that he wrote it simply enough for the local church to understand. Paul's letters, like entire Bible, are simple and yet sublime. It's true of Shakespeare's plays and nearly all the Great Books of the Western World. Peter admits he understands the basic message of Paul. Peter is spiritual enough. The rest, the hard stuff, may be clarified in a number of ways.

Just like any document Paul's Letters have a context. If you read something without knowing the recipient of the letter and the circumstances, you won't understand the whole thing. That's true of Paul's letters as well as the four Gospels. Each gospel was written for a different purpose in mind.

Content also has a context. Look at 1 Corinthians 11:2-16. What exactly is the *head covering*? Some Catholic and

Episcopal Church women wear veils on their heads when they enter the church. The Greek text is sometimes translated into *veil*. Verse 15 suggests that the covering is not made of cloth, but is a woman's long hair. We are not even sure if Paul is just taking about women in general or married women. I have my own idea. In the Corinthian community, married women wear their hair up. Some of them, perhaps while they are speaking in the language of angels, are letting down their hair. They think that they are so spiritual that they are caught up into the heavenly realms where we are *neither married nor given in marriage* (Matthew 22:30, 1 Corinthians 11:10). But to let down their hair during worship in the Corinthian culture suggests that either their husbands are dead or they are like prostitutes who have many, many husbands (John 4:16-18).

Is my interpretation correct? I could be wrong. But the main principle of 1 Corinthians 11:2-16 is easy enough to understand. The relationship between God and man must be honored. There is a relationship of equality and submission in the male and female relationship. That relationship must be honored in our worship to God. In the history of the Holy Spirit's work in the church, there has been no unity in defining *head cover*. To presume that there is some spiritual answer is presumptuous.

In the matter of the Second Coming, the Scripture is clear about some things. But others are not. It's clear that Jesus is coming again. Events, cataclysmic events, happening even now are foretelling His coming. The Bible calls them *labor pains*. You can't know which one is the last, but you know the baby is coming (Hosea 13:13; Matt. 24:8; Mark 13:8; Rom. 8:22; 1 Thess. 5:3). Amen!

Is my interpretation of the Genesis creation correct? I could be wrong. Maybe I want my Bible to be as specific as my ninth grade biology book. Even in Jesus' day, the Jews did not entirely agree with interpreting the length of days. Even before scientific discoveries appeared, the church was not entirely in agreement about how long those days were. Watchman Nee seemed to accept unquestionably the creation teachings of Victorian apologeticist G. H. Pember* because he gave structure to Nee's belief in human nature. Was a single day even longer than a thousand years (Ps. 90:4)? Or was it 24 hours? As you read the Psalms and Revelation, its seems like God does not want to give us all the answers about how He did it. He wants worship. He wants us to go out look at the landscape and the starry night, and praise him for being such a Great Creator. He wants us to be in wonder at the thought that there is a new and better creation already entering history in Jesus Christ, the Second Adam. *The last days* are actually the first days of a new creation. The last day of the old creation saw the first man. The first day of the new creation sees a new Adam. Revelation 22 tells that there will be a new Heaven and earth.

The Bible is not just for people who have to do intense "spiritual" gymnastics to shed their carnal nature. The basic message is clear enough for even children to understand (Deuteronomy 6:6-7). That truth is clearly visible in the hearts of Sunday school children and among the so-called handicapped. Aaron understands the meaning of the Bible. He is an adult with Down's syndrome living in Florida. Because he had two adoptive parents who patiently loved him, he can read, and even better than I, he knows how

---

* G. H. Pember (1837-1910) had quite an imagination. He provided his era warning about the dangers of spiritism, but he missed the mark when it come to evidence. He believed that Chinese Buddhists had converted the Indians. Pember may have known a lot about the English Bible, but he knew little about history, Buddhism, or Native Americans. Like the *Book of Mormon*'s speculations on the Native Americans, there is not one piece of evidence to support the idea. The Bible, especially, 1 Corinthians 15:3-8, expects a higher standard evidence.

much God loves him. I know of another, older child of God just like him who was raised by godly Catholic Christian parents. His mind is too simple to turn his back on God. As the next chapter will show, they are spiritual men.

Chapter 3 Endnotes

1. Karl Barth, *Church Dogmatics*, 4 vols., gen. eds. G.W. Bromily and T.F. Torrance (Edinburgh: T. and T. Clark, 1936-62), vol. 1: *The Doctrine of the Word of God: Prolegomena to Church Dogmatics*, 2 Parts (1936, 1956), trans. G.T. Thomson and H. Knight, 2:528ff.

2. Ibid., 1:98-140.

3. Nee, *The Ministry*, p. 11.

4. Ibid., p. 14.

5. Barth, *Doctrine of the Word*, 2:528ff.

6. Ibid., 1:123ff.

7. Nee, *Living Sacrifice*, p. 67.

8. Nee, *Search*, p. 12.

9. Ibid., p. 13.

10. 1 Corinthians 2:13. See Nee, *Search*, pp. 17-23.

11. Nee, *The Ministry*, pp. 83-84.

12. Idem, *Search*, p. 15.

13. Idem, *The Ministry*, p. 60.

14. Idem, *Search*, p. 20.

15. Arthur T. Pierson, *The Bible and Spiritual Criticism*, reprint ed. (Grand Rapids: Baker Book House Company, 1970), p. 15.

16. Nee, *Search*, pp. 43-90.

17. See pp. 148ff. below.

18. Nee, *The Ministry*, p. 115.

19. Ibid., p. 103.

20. Idem, *Sit, Walk, Stand*, 4th ed., rev. (Fort Washington, Pa.: Christian Literature Crusade, 1962), p. 11. Cf. idem, *Christian Life*, pp. 40ff.

21. Idem, *The Ministry*, p. 124.

22. Idem, *Spiritual Man*, 2:10ff.; *The Ministry*, p. 131.

23. Idem, *Spiritual Man*, 1:28; *Gospel Dialogue* (New York: Christian Fellowship Publishers, 1975), pp. 106-9.

24. Idem, *Spiritual Knowledge* (New York: Christian Fellowship Publishers, Inc., 1973), pp. 65-82; *The Ministry*, pp. 143-45; *Christ: The Sum*, pp. 47-54; *God's Work* (New York: Christian Fellowship Publishers, 1974), pp. 17-24. See John 8:12 and other passages on "light."

25. Idem, *The Ministry*, p. 143.

26. Ibid., p. 144.

27. Idem, *The Spiritual Man*, 3:64-65.

28. Idem, *The Ministry*, p. 146.

29. Idem, *Knowledge*, p. 11.

30. Idem, *The Ministry*, p. 151; see also pp. 28, 29, 33, 39, 109, 146, 150-56, 180, 213, 218, 223-25, 263, and 266.

31. Ibid., p. 159. The word is incorrectly transliterated as "massam" in the English translation.

32. Ibid., p. 170.

33. Ibid., pp. 180-81.

34. Ibid., pp. 197ff. Cf. John 14:26.

35. Ibid., p. 208.

36. Ibid., p. 220.

37. Ibid., p. 227.

38. Ibid., pp. 245ff.

39. Ibid., p. 246.

40. Ibid., p. 281.

41. Ibid., p. 45.

42. Lee, *Christ vs. Religion*, pp. 32-33.

43. Much of the ideas in this paragraph come from Wayne Grudem's *Systematic Theology* (Grand Rapids: Zondervan Books, 1995), Part One, Chapter 6: *Clarity*.

44. See especially Watchman Nee. *The Mystery of Creation* (New York: Christian Fellowship Publishers, Inc., 1974), p. 13. Neither G. H. Pember or Watchman Nee knew Hebrew. Both of them taught that Genesis 1:2 should be translated "The earth *became* waste" instead of "The earth *was* waste." They taught that the verse proves that only Genesis 1:1 speaks of an earlier creation. But the verb can not be translated as *became* without an additional preposition. Using a Hebrew Lexicon without knowledge of Grammar can also be a waste of a time.

CHAPTER FOUR

Nee's Anthropology:
The Spiritual Man and His Life

C Ryder Smith, in his book *The Biblical Doctrine of Man*, reconstructs a biblical theology of man according to the New and Old Testaments' response to two paramount questions: "What is a man?" and "What ought a man to be?"[1] It is the latter question, which becomes the central theme of all of Watchman Nee's writings. He hypothesizes that the ills of the church can be traced to its failure to correctly answer this anthropological/theological question. From the beginning of his ministry, he considered it his special task "to give God's children a clear understanding of spiritual life in order that the Holy Spirit might use it [*The Spiritual Man*] in leading the saints onward and in delivering them from groping in darkness."[2] While his multivolume work, *The Spiritual Man*, is the single most comprehensive statement of his doctrine of man, *Spiritual Reality or Obsession, The Latent Power of the Soul, The Release of the Spirit*, and *The Normal Christian Life* are equally important studies on anthropology. The content of this chapter will deal with the specific principles developed in these five works.

The Trinity of Man

Theological speculation within the church on the constitutional nature of man has divided into two lines of thought. Trichotomists hold that man is the unity of the human spirit (*ruach/pneuma*), soul (*nephesh/psuchē*), and body (beten, geviyyah/sōma). The dichotomists affirm the presence of an immaterial nature comprising both soul and spirit that reposes in the material element of the body of flesh. In the patristic age support was divided[3] on this as they attempted to theologize on the origin of the soul, the nature of immortality, and the resurrection, and the problem of sin in the life of the believer. While the Western Church has historically supported the dichotomous view, some have doubted whether this view is entirely applicable to the dynamics of the Christian life.

The critical, scientific age of the post-Reformation era presented new problems that required a further examination of the biblical perception of the human framework. William Harvey's study of the human heart (1616) revealed that this organ was a pump and not the seat of the human will. The heart and the entire body could therefore be examined and "healed" by the nonspiritual eye of the lay physician. James G. Frazer's study of comparative religion and culture, Franz Anton Mesmer's discovery of "personal magnetism," Freudian psychology, and the parallel rise of the "Higher Life" Movement[4] created an intellectual climate suitable for a reworking of historical trichotomy and its intrapsychic dynamics.

Prior to his period, for example, the dichotomous approach had interpreted "spiritual warfare" as a battle between the flight of the soul to God and the inordinate passions of the human body. But the new trichotomy, far less cosmologically dualistic, concerned itself with the spiritual battle described in the Keswick interpretation of Rom. 5:12-

8:17.[5] Here the presence of the "double I" in 7:14-25 and the contrast between the mind set on things of the flesh and the mind set on things of the spirit necessitated a more distinct, trichotomous bifurcation of the nonphysical elements of man. This interpretation of the tripartite construction of man is most apparent in the writings of J.B. Heard, Mary E. McDonough, Andrew Murray, G.H. Pember, Jessie Penn-Lewis, A.T. Pierson, and Watchman Nee.[6]

But there is another interpretation. It is an interpretation more favored by people whose studies focus on understanding how the Bible was understood in the biblical era. They don't try to decide how biblical Calvin, Thomas Aquinas, Watchman Nee, or C. S. Lewis is. They try to understand how the Bible was understood in Bible times. They study Greek and Hebrew cultures. They study the various ways Greek and Hebrew words were used.

The Third view sees both the dichotomous and the trichotomous as too Greek and less biblical. The Greeks gave us the word, *atom*, the smallest part of the earth. They gave us the words, *anatomical* and *analysis*. The Greek idea was to dissect everything down into parts. The person is made of two parts or three parts. But to the Hebrew mind, you are a whole person, a living soul. People are either alive or dead. It is God's breath or Spirit that makes us alive. You have to have both a body and a spirit to be alive. The word, *spirit*, means "the whole man." *Soul* means "the whole man." But the former word reminds us that we need God to live. The whole man is spiritual. Gifts from God are spiritual. God's law is spiritual because God's will and power descend and work through them. Carnal or soulical is the whole man setting his life upon what is terminal and in a state of decay.

To live or act a life apart from God is to be carnal. It is also foolish. If the branch removes itself from the vine, its future is only death and decay. Christians have been saved by the most spiritual event in history. It is not something worldly, done without God's help. Christians have every reason to walk in the Spirit. We have been immersed/baptized in the Holy Spirit. Our new life is eternally connected to Christ the vine. Yet, as Paul reminds us in 1 Corinthians that though we are spiritual, we can act in a carnal or worldly manner.

To be spiritual does not mean we use one part of soul/ mind/spirit and not another. To be spiritual means to do things for the glory of God:

> "Never be lacking in zeal, but keep your spiritual fervor, serving the Lord. Be joyful in hope, patient in affliction, faithful in prayer" (Romans 12:11).

> "So whether you eat or drink or whatever you do, do it all for the glory of God" (1 Corinthians 10:31).

Our actions are spiritual when they respond to the grace of God. Paul calls them "the fruit of the Spirit." Spiritual fruit are actions or attitudes derived from our living relationship with God through Jesus Christ.

Is it the fruit of the spirit? Is it fruit of the Spirit with a capital "T"? It may be both. How can they be both? I don't know. How can Jesus be both fully man and fully God? I don't know. God raised Jesus body and soul. No dichotomy there. Our bodies will also be resurrected. Before the second resurrection, the dead are given temporary bodies to dwell in Heaven.

What does such a whole-man view mean for our Christian life? It means that 1) many religious things can be done in a worldly manner, and 2) many secular things can be done in a spiritual manner.

1. Sally Smith attends Wednesday Bible study, Saturday night prayer meeting, and Sunday morning worship and

witnesses to her neighbors on Tuesday Outreach. As she listens to Wednesday's anointed teaching she thought about her husband: "He is so unspiritual. I don't know why I ever married him. Why couldn't he be like Pastor Jones?"

2. That same night Shirley Richter didn't attend Bible study. She decided to stay home and cook her husband his favorite foods. She's forty-eight and her husband is fifty-three. She wishes she was ten pounds lighter, and he still needs to lose another fifteen. She called him at work and told him to come right home. She set candles on the table. He brought flowers. Later that evening, he gave her a kiss and said, "Everyday I thank God for you." He turned out the lights and she said, "Me too."

Outwardly, Sally is more spiritual. And yet, which woman brings more glory to God? Sometimes the answer seems so obvious and yet the Bible says, "… judge nothing before the appointed time; wait till the Lord comes. He will bring to light what is hidden in darkness and will expose the motives of men's hearts. At that time each will receive his praise from God" (1 Cor. 4:3).

Within the laws of God, everything we do can be *spiritual*. Eating a meal; playing with your children; spending a quiet, romantic evening with your spouse; and attending a Bible study are all spiritual as long as they glorify God and are not intended to add to your own sense of pride.

At the very beginning of Watchman Nee's book *The Spiritual Man*, he patently expresses his full support for a trichotomous position:

> The ordinary concept of the constitution of human beings is dualistic—soul and body. According to this concept, soul is the invisible inner spiritual part, while body is the visible outer corporal part. Though there is some truth to this, it is nevertheless inaccurate. Such an opinion comes from fallen man, not from God; apart from

God's revelation, no concept is dependable. That the body is man's outward sheath is undoubtedly correct, but the Bible never confuses spirit and soul as though they are the same. Not only are they different in terms; their very nature differs from each other. The Word of God does not divide man into two parts of soul and body. It treats man, rather, as tripartite—spirit, soul and body. 1 Thessalonians 5:23 reads: "May the God of peace himself sanctify you wholly; and may your spirit and soul and body be kept sound and blameless at the coming of our Lord Jesus Christ." This verse precisely shows that the whole man is divided into three parts.[7]*

Nee goes on by saying that the dividing of soul and spirit is of "supreme importance"[8] to spiritual growth and maturity. In Heb. 4:12, he sees the Word of God dividing our soul from our spirit. Analogous with the temple sacrifice that is divided by the priest's sword, Jesus divides us into three parts as the believer offers himself upon the altar of God.[9]

The Creation and Fall of Man

In most theologies that attempt to vindicate a three-part description of man, the Adamic creation account in Gen. 2:7 appears as a central text.[10] Watchman Nee is no exception.[11] Quite consistent with other trichotomous writers of his age, Nee sees the prefallen Adamic nature as a merging of spirit and body to form a third part—the human soul. While the angels are called "spirits," and animals have souls and bodies, only man is made in the tridimensional image of God: "A complete man is a trinity—the composite of spirit, soul, and body."[12]

Somewhat like the divine trinity, Nee ascribes a specific function for each human part.[13] The corporal body is most

---

* Here his concern is not so much with those who see the spirit as a functionally distinct unit, equal to the mind or heart, within the soul. Rather, Nee objects to a dualism, which considers spirit and soul as synonymous with the human psyche. See pp. 98ff., "The Soul."

clearly aligned to material reality and gives man his "world-consciousness." The soul, with its intellect and emotions, "belongs to man's own self and reveals his personality. It is termed as the part with 'self-consciousness.'"[14] The spirit apprehends, communes with and worships God, and is the element of "God-consciousness." Taking his cue from Scripture references on an "inner" and "outward" man,[15] the three elements in his personality theory can be accurately depicted in this way:

Man's Tripartite Being[16]

In this model it is clear that the soul occupies an important mediating position in determining whether Adam' outward actions conform to the inner witness of God's spirit.

As the product of the corporal and pneumatic union, the human soul is superior to the animal soul. It is the organ of man's free will, wherein his full potential as a servant of God or a doer of evil is realized. Before the fall, the soul was a steward of the spirit and could have become morally and spiritually in the image and likeness of God. On the basis of an apparent delegation of authority in Gen. 1:27-28, Nee believes Adam's soul was given tremendous power:

Although we may not rate Adam's power as being a billion times over ours, we can nonetheless safely reckon it to be a million times over ours. Else he would have not been able to perform the duty commanded him of God. As for us today, though, if we were required to merely sweep a lane three times daily, we would not be able afterwards to straighten our back. How then could we possibly rule the earth? Yet, Adam not only ruled the earth, but he also had dominion over the fish of the sea, the birds of the heavens, and every living thing on earth. To rule is not just to sit by doing nothing. It requires management and work. From a seeing of this we should recognize the superior power, which Adam in fact possessed. It far exceeds our present situation.[17]

The body was likewise bestowed with immortality, incorruptibility, and perfect health upon the condition of his obedience to God. His spirit and soul would then maintain the body in its created state forever without change.[18]

Each part of man was tremendously endowed by God and as such, followed a proper hierarchy according to the Creator's will. The spirit was given the highest part of man's being, to which soul and body were subject:

> Under normal conditions, the spirit is like a mistress, the soul like a steward, and the body like a servant. The mistress commits matters to the steward, who in turn commands the servant to carry them out. The mistress gives orders privately to the steward; the steward in turn transmits them openly to the servant. The steward appears to be Lord of all, but in actuality, the Lord over all is the mistress.[19]

In the Genesis narration, two special trees have been set in the Garden of Eden: the tree of life and the tree of the knowledge of good and evil. Nee sees in the two trees a "two-way" tradition. The former germinates the way of the spirit, and the eating of its fruit is unrestricted. The latter develops the way of the soul, and its fruit is forbidden. At this point man was in a state of innocence and so to speak was "morally neutral—neither sinful nor holy."[20]

Simultaneously he had the free will to assimilate either the fruit of spiritual life or the fruit of the soulical life. In a sense the two trees offered him a choice whether he would become a self-sufficient man, capable of deciding moral issues, or whether he would become dependent on God's judgment of right and wrong, partaking even of the life of God:

Thus, he would become a "son" of God, in the sense of having in him a life that derived from God. There you would have God's life in union with man: a race of men having the life of God in them and living in constant dependence upon God for that life. But if instead Adam should turn the other way, and take of the tree of the knowledge of good and evil, then he would develop his own manhood along natural lines apart from God. As a self-sufficient being, he would possess in himself the power to form independent judgment, but he would have no life in God.[21]

The history of mankind has shown the outcome of that choice. Apart from grace, humanity is self-dependent, judging, and acting without God. The serpent offered Adam greater power of the soul/self-consciousness through the knowledge of good and evil. In so doing Adam believed that the chasm between God's power and his own soul power could be breeched and he could be as a god.

In the fall,* Adam disobeyed God's loving admonition, and this sin separated him from God's presence. The proper order of the human trilogy is disturbed. The soul ceases to be a steward of the spirit, and its power is "frozen" or immobilized. The soul is now puffed-up intellectually† to the degree that the spirit is deflated to the point of becoming

---

* Nee also describes the temptation of Eve as an attack, first upon the needs of the body (eat), then of the soul (knowledge), and finally reaching her spirit (open rebellion against God).[22]

† "Because the fall of man was occasioned by seeking knowledge, God uses the foolishness of the cross to 'destroy the wisdom of the wise.'"[23]

dead in its sensitivity and activity toward God (Gen. 2:17).[24] Adam's body, barred from the tree of life and an immortal life with God, bears the mark of mortality, suffers pain and sickness, and is under the reign of sin.

By the original sin all humanity suffers and must await the restoration through Christ, the second Adam. Original sin is our inheritance at birth and is a life of the soul marked by the dominion of the flesh. Such a life is centered on and often succumbs to the carnal needs of the body. Apart from the revelation of the law the unregenerate is even unconscious of being utterly sinful and corrupt.[25] His power and strength are not from God as received through the human spirit, but from the fallen soulical nature, devoid of any spiritual sense.

As prince of this world, the devil's intent is to accuse and stir up this independent power. His purpose is to gain further control over man. Nee is convinced that this fallen and independent power of man provides much of the metaphysical dynamics of religious obsessions, cults, heresies, and other religions.

Regardless of the unregenerate state of even the prophets,* God has fashioned the Old Testament revelation in such a way as to reveal the proper order of human nature: spirit, soul and body. In addition to Gen. 2:7, Nee lists a number of Old Testament passages in which he sees a scission in the role of the spirit and the role of the soul.[26] Nee is at least aware of the criticism that other passages† suggest that the Hebrew term for "soul" and "spirit" are synonymous. He concludes that the Old Testament disparity of the evidence also reveals that the unregenerate spirit, under the dominion of sin and death, functions semantically like the overpowering

---

* See pp. 61-62, 69.

† Particularly, Gen. 41:8; Judg. 8:3; Prov. 14:29;17:22; Isa. 29:24; 65:14; Dan. 5:20.[27]

soul. "Before the believer is born again," Nee retorts, "his spirit becomes so sunken and surrounded by his soul that it is impossible for him to distinguish whether something is emanating from the soul or from the spirit."[28]

Even the Christian, due to long years of "soulical" bondage, knows very little of his spirit and must seek teaching through revelation and experience of what is soulish and what is spiritual. Nee feels it to be his ministry to recover this truth for the churches of God.[29]

An important Old Testament image for a tripartite humanity is found in the design of the temple. Taking Paul's comment in 1 Corinthians 3:16 as a hermeneutical base, Nee sees direct functional relationships between the body and the outer court, the soul and the Holy Place, and the spirit and the Holy of Holies.[30] Like the body, the outer court is the place of external worship, and its life is visible to all. In the Holy Place the priest presents himself and his offering to God. Similarly, the soul is the inner life of man, where he may offer up his emotions, volition, and mind to God. The Holy of Holies is the dwelling place of God and cannot be reached by man unless the veil is rent. Its purpose parallels that of the spirit, where man unites and communes with God.

Christ: The Sum of All Spiritual Things

While the Old Covenant was set in the economy/dispensation of the law and the promise, it is in the New Covenant of Christ's ministry that the restoration to completeness of spiritual life begins and ends. Christ is the promised redeemer. For, as a result of the sin that permeates spirit, soul and body, the spiritual death that has separated man from God has spread to all men. No self-improvement theology of salvation can change this:

> Death has permeated the spirit, soul, and body of all
> men; there is no part of a human being into which it has

not found its way. It is therefore imperative that man receives God's life. The way of salvation cannot be in human reform, for "death" is irreparable. Sin must be judged before there can be rescue out of death.[31]

Since sin has wrought death to the entire man, Christ's atonement through death is a death through His entire triune nature.[32] His physical suffering atoned for sins conducted by the body. By refusing a sedative (wine mingled with myrrh),* He also refused to lose consciousness, to atone for the will in man's soul. In many ways He had been humiliated and thereby further atoned for man's soul. But His greatest suffering was spiritual in that He was abandoned by God (cf. Matt. 27:46).

In a number of references, Nee speaks of the believer's identification with Christ's death, and His death is reckoned as our death.[34] From that point on, the work of translating man into the image of God can begin. At the same time that he has died with Christ, the believer is raised into newness of life and receives a new human spirit from God. As the temple needs the Holy of Holies to be the tabernacle or dwelling place of God, so also man receives a new spirit that becomes a dwelling place of God's Spirit.

Unlike Andrew Murray, Nee preached that the reception of the Holy Spirit is not experienced in a second work of grace, but is part of the believer's initial salvation event.[35] But like many expositors of the Pentecostal or Holiness doctrines on the Spirit, Nee felt that conversion is not the only experience in what he called "the normal Christian life." Four experiences are listed and described, each of which begins with a further, "objective" revelation of Christ and the cross.[36] For each stage is only a further realization of the

---

* There is some debate whether the "wine mingled with myrrh" mentioned in Mark 15:23 is a sedative or a local beverage. See n. 33.

depth of human weakness and of the depth and scope of our need of union and identification in the death and resurrection of Christ:

> What we need to comprehend before God is that our experience there is neither thing nor affair, but only Christ: not that He gives us light, but that He is our light; not that He leads the way, but He is the way; not that He gives us a life, but He is our life; not that He teaches a truth, but He is truth. Brethren, do you grasp the difference here? Whatever Christ gives is His very own self.[37]

Every enlightenment starts with more knowledge of Christ, because "God's Christ is all things; aside from Him, God has nothing."[38] The four experiences are "justification and the new birth," "deliverance from sin," "the gift of the Holy Spirit," and "pleasing God." Subjectively, each serves as a further step in the believer's walk with the Lord, as both a crisis and a process of growth.

The importance of this growth process in Nee's theology has thus far been overlooked. Yet the steps comprise much of the meaning and content of *The Spiritual Man* and *The Normal Christian Life*. In the former Nee describes Christian growth in terms of his tripartite formula of spirit, soul, and body. In the latter, produced some ten years later, growth structure is presented in terms of the Keswick interpretation of Roman 5-8 and the work of the cross. In both, the basic purpose or aim of the message is to provide guidance for those who wish to be "overcomers" of the world and their fallen human natures. It is nothing less than the victorious Christian life.

At the very base of these four graces of spiritual life is his detailed understanding of the tripartite being. For every work of the cross in the life of the believer strengthens or counteracts some aspect or characteristic of the spirit, soul or body that hinders the effectual implementation of the

Christian walk with God. Because of the extent of the reconstruction of man, two works of grace are not enough; four responses to revelation are necessary. The rest of this chapter will first look at Nee's descriptive profile of the inner workings of man and then will examine how they are affected by Nee's four works of grace.

PLEASE NOTE: There's a secret about Nee's interpretation of the trichotomous man. That will be explained later.

Spirit

One of the fundamental principles of Watchman Nee's theology is that the spirit is the place where the regenerated man works together with God.[39] Within his regenerated spirit lie all the works of God towards him, and he must not mistake its activity with that of the soul. The Holy Spirit resides there and first reveals and applies the finished work of the cross to the believer. As he states, "God's aim in a regenerated man is for that man by his spirit to rid himself of everything belonging to the old creation, because within his regenerated spirit lie all the works of God towards him."[40]

As the organ of God-consciousness, the Christian must realize he has a spirit. If he does, he can understand the meaning of the cross, resist the flesh and pray "with all perseverance until the answer comes."[41] His service to God will not be subject to his emotions, or the cleverness of his mind, or the strength of his will, but only to the will of God. If he is unconscious of his own spirit and its activities, his spirit may become defiled, and his ministry will not honor and glorify the Lord.

In addition to realizing that we have a spirit, Nee is concerned that the believer should understand and assimilate the laws of the spirit that are necessary for the spiritual walk. Knowledge of these laws comes only as one gets acquainted with the different functions that are distinctive to the spirit's work.[42] In his analysis of the spirit he lists three main functions: intuition, communion, and conscience. In keeping with his typological emphasis, Nee metaphorically compares these functions with the Ark of the Covenant in the Holy of Holies.[43] Within the ark lies the law of God; by the spirit's intuition God makes His will and Himself known. The mercy seat upon the ark manifests God's glory and receives a worship offering of blood; in communion man's blood-cleansed spirit worships and converses with the living God. The ark is the "Ark of Testimony" in that the two tablets of the law silently accused or excused Israel's actions; the believer's conscience also bears witness for or against his conduct.

Intuition

"Intuition" serves as the sense organ of the spirit, for it responds directly to the things beyond human understanding or cause.* Contrary to all rational and discernible evidence, the intuition may speak out with "an unuttered and soundless voice" strongly opposing decisions conceived by the outward man. Nee is concerned that the believer be diligent to distinguish the inner voice from any outer feelings.

Intuition receives the anointing that teaches:

> You have been anointed by the Holy One, and you all know ... But the anointing which you received from him abides in you, and you have no need that any one should teach you; as his anointing teaches you about everything, and is true, and is no lie, just as it has taught you, abide in him.[45]

This "anointing" brings us into a sense of knowledge of spiritual things. It is not the same thing as a mental

---

* Nee cites the following biblical texts as evidence of the human intuition: Matt. 26:41; Mark 2:8; 8:12; Luke 1:47; John 4:23; 11:33; 13:21; Acts 17:16; 18:25; 19:21; 20:22; Rom. 12:11; 1 Corinthians 2:11; 14:15-16; 2 Corinthians 2:13; 4:13; Eph. 1:17; Col. 1:8.[44]

understanding, and Nee is quick to point out the difference and division of the two. Human understanding rests upon intellectual accomplishment, whereas "knowing" by the spirit is a non-rational assurance in matters of faith that cannot be directly communicated to others.

One of the ways in which this "anointing of the spirit" helps is in the area of discerning the truth from lies and "what is of Christ from what is of the antichrists."[46] Without discernment, Nee concludes, only a Christian with a good mind and education would escape deception. While Nee nowhere suggests that the Christian faith is irrational or logically inconsistent with itself, he does feel that the believer's first bulwark against deception is the intuitive "small voice."[47]

In dealing with people, the Christian's spirit can give unmistakable discernment about certain individuals. Investigation through inquiry and observation can occupy only a second place in understanding people. Such methods are insensitive to the human heart and therefore cannot be used as the primary tool to evaluate people. As an example of such intuitive understanding, Nee remarks on a child's gift in accurately understanding people and Jesus' discernment of the scribes in Mark 2:8. Such childlikeness and Christlikeness, Nee remarks, "ought to be the normal condition of every spiritual person."[48]

In the previous chapter of this book, dealing with "The Word and Its Ministry," it was noted that Nee believed in the continuing revelation in the man who has received the basic revelation/light of salvation.[49] It is in his intuition that man receives that light:

> To know things in our intuition is what the Bible calls revelation. Revelation has no other meaning than that the Holy Spirit enables a believer to apprehend a particular matter by indicating the reality of it to his spirit. There is but one kind of knowledge concerning either the Bible or

God, which is valuable, and that is the truth revealed to our spirit by God's spirit.[50]

He is quick to add that it must be distinguished or divided from certain special experiences or intellectual comprehension:

> This kind of revelation is not a vision, a heavenly voice, a dream, or an external force, which shakes the man. One may encounter these phenomena and still not have revelation. Revelation happens in the intuition—quietly, neither hastily nor slowly, soundless and yet with a message. How many denominate themselves Christians, though the Christianity they embrace is simply a kind of philosophy of life or of ethics, a few articles of truth, or some supernatural manifestations. Such an attitude will issue neither in a new birth nor a new spirit. Numerous are these "Christians" whose spiritual usefulness measures up to zero. Not so are those who have received Christ, for by the grace of God they have perceived in their spirit the reality of the spiritual realm, which opens to them like the lifting of a veil. What they today know is far more profound than what their mind has comprehended; yea, it seems as though a new meaning has been imparted to all, which they had only understood or comprehended in the past.[51]

Since the believer's life is characterized by two-way communication, there are two kinds of revelation in our spirit: the direct and the sought. In direct revelation God has a particular wish for the believer and reveals it through a regenerate spirit. In "sought revelation" the less mature believer seeks an answer to a specific need and awaits an answer through God's movement in his spirit.[52] The sum total of both kinds of revelation received within the individual's spirit is the entire content of his spiritual knowledge.[53] Nee warns that no amount or argument, reason or contemplation can add to it. Although the mind has value secondarily, any experience arising out of it is from man himself and does not come through intuition, man's spiritual sense organ.

Communion

The second function of the spirit is communion. As defined in the second volume of *The Spiritual Man*, it is not at first apparent whether a real distinction exists between intuition and communion. Nee even begins his analysis of communion by identifying it as an intuitive faculty. But as further defined, communion is the activity of receiving the revelation of God through one's intuition.[54] If the Christian remains spiritual, his intuition is alive, and he will enjoy uninterrupted communion with God. Worship does enter into the communion relationship, but Nee's emphasis is more towards communion as apprehension of spiritual knowledge and understanding. He seems to steer clear of any type of balanced presentation of an I-Thou understanding of communion. For the believer to speak his mind in prayer is considered rather superficial and immature by Nee.[55] Christians are rather to set their worship to the cognition of the mind of God:

> Many devotional prayers, prayers of fellowship, and prayers of request cannot be a substitute for prayer as ministry or work. If all our prayers are simply devotional or merely consist of fellowshipping and asking, our prayer is *too small*. Prayer as work or ministry means that we stand on God's side, desiring what He desires. To pray according to God's will is a most powerful thing. For the church to pray signifies that she has discovered God's will and is now voicing it. Prayer is not only asking God, it is also the making of a declaration. As the church prays, she stands on God's side and declares that what man wants is what He wants. If the church should so declare, the declaration will be at once effectual. [Italics mine.][56*]

Any prayer that does come from the mind (1 Corinthians 14:15) must have its content originate from the revelation of the spirit.

---

* Like Wesley, Nee seems to be making a distinction between deliberate and indeliberate sins.[60]

Conscience

The final function of the spirit is conscience. It corrects and reprimands when men fall short of the glory of God. It expresses the holiness of God and is extremely important in the life of the believer and nonbeliever as well. While the unbeliever's spirit is dead, the death of the conscience is not as deep as* that of communion. Hence the conscience can arise out of its comatose state to accuse even the unregenerate. But without communion with God, his conscience cannot reveal the eternal, spiritual life to him.[57]

For a believer has been quickened at his rebirth, and he is consequently more sensitive to sin. Once he transgresses God's ordinances, the conscience immediately testifies that he is not clear towards God and towards men. Invariably the believer will repent or quench its protest by arguing or trying to appease it with a show of good works.[58]

The spiritual man hears the voice of conscience and allows the Holy Spirit to point out every one of his sins. Confessing his sins, he trusts in the precious blood of Christ for cleansing and continually seeks the will of God in his life. Inseparable from his great faith, he has a good conscience (cf. 1 Tim. 1:5, 19) and therefore can freely converse with God.[59] Finally his conscience assures him that as far as his spiritual knowledge goes, he has arrived at the immediate goal of perfection, a foretaste of his eschatological completion in the resurrection.

A believer with a weak conscience has a different ethic by which to live than a man with a good conscience.[61] The freedom in Christ of a believer with a weak conscience is limited according to the level of grace he has thus far experienced in his life. While another man may have a clear

---

*Nee appears to have modified his stand near the end of his ministry. See *Living Sacrifice*, pp. 82-97.

conscience to eat meat offered to idols (as in 1 Corinthians 8-10), his conscience is disturbed. He has not yet come to know the full meaning of the cross and his liberty in the New Covenant. To go against his conscience now would be for him and for God an act of willful disobedience.

In his analysis, Nee stresses the point that all three functions of the spirit are "intertwined."[62] As such it is essential to the life of the spirit that each function should be carried out according to the work of the Holy Spirit. If one function is hindered or suffers, the entire spirit is affected.

Laws of the Spirit

Once the believer understands that his spirit must be intuitively open to revelation, be in communion with God, and have a clear conscience, he can appreciate the laws of the spirit. Nee lists eight laws of the spirit (italics added):

1) The spirit needs to be kept in a state of perfect freedom.[63] The believer may often sense oppression and heaviness weighing upon his spiritual life. Nee warns that such a sensation is an attack of Satan to dull his spiritual sense to the degree that it hinders the work of God. If encountered in the morning, the whole day will be a loss to him and to the church. Nee admonishes the church to deal with oppression of the spirit immediately:

> The way to handle it is to stop the work at hand at once, set your will against this weight, and exercise your spirit to oppose it. Occasionally you may have to utter words audibly against it; at other times with the power of your spirit you should resist in prayer.[64]

One must also attempt to uncover the cause behind his oppression. Through spiritual discernment, he will see some failure on his part to cooperate with God at a particular time with regard to a particular matter.

2) *The spirit requires the soul and body as the organ of its expression.*[65] In this maxim Nee states that one requirement for a normal expression of the spirit is a normal soul and body. When these parts cease to serve as the spirit's outlet, the believer loses his "aliveness," is bashful, and the public proclamation of his faith becomes hidden. Release comes through the exercise of his will in prayer and the declaration of the victorious name of the Lord Jesus over every onslaught of the enemy. Without his own prayers and the prayers of others, he will continue to show the symptoms of spiritual suffocation until the outward man is broken.

3) *The spirit can be broken through sorrow, grief, anguish, or heartbreak.*[66] Such emotions may not be elicited through the spirit and may be regarded as an attack of Satan. Such attacks of depression can create in us a number of abnormal symptoms. The Christian may become stiff, unyielding, narrow, and selfish. Under his personality, the whole church may become just as unforgiving, sectarian, and prideful as he is. The poisoning of his spirit colors his speaking and must be dealt with quickly:

> The moment we notice our voice has turned harsh, we must stop instantly. With not the slightest hesitation we should turn to ourselves and say, "I am willing to speak with a pure spirit; I am willing to oppose the enemy." If we are reluctant to say to our brethren, "I am wrong," then our spirit remains engulfed in its sin.[67]

As a preventive, Nee encourages the believer to recognize faith as a shield against these "darts" of Satan.[68]

4) *The spirit "sinking or being submerged" into the soul is largely due to a turning in on oneself.*[69] Nee provides four symptoms of this "sinking" of the spirit. If he is possessive over all his spiritual experiences, if he has an intrusion of the power of darkness in his life, if his prayer and worship is self-centered, or if he dwells in "physical sensations and

---

Watchman Nee on Depression

What is this "sinking" that Nee is describing? It sounds like depression. Nee lived at a time when medical knowledge in China was limited. Nee even says, "If one does not have God's Word, he needs to abide by the law of sanitation. But if one has God's Word, he can afford to be an extremist, fearing nothing."[71] We now know that depression is a clear example of the unity between our thinking and our body. Poor diet, exhaustion, anxiety, and a number of other mental and physical causes can create depression. When Jesus was at Gethsemane he was "exceedingly sorrowful." Some of the greatest Christian poets and writers suffered from this malady of the mind/body.

---

various wonderful experiences" supplied by Satan, his spirit is most certainly sinking.[70] If the sinking continues, Nee even says, "He may perhaps be possessed by the evil spirit." To prevent the spirit from any further sinking in the soul, the believer's spirit must flow out. Only when the spirit is directed outward can the believer's spirit be restored to its original state.

5) *"The burden of the spirit differs from the weights on the spirit."* The former issues from God, and the freedom of prayer is never lost; the latter is an oppression from Satan that inhibits prayer.[72]

6) *God's life and power in the spirit can recede like a tide.*[73] This law is a corollary to law number two. For the recession of God's life is not God's fault, but is the result of an obstructed outlet. The signs of this condition are given in some detail and appear to describe the actual experience of many believers:

Day by day, he grows weaker. At this time, he seems to lose his taste for communion with God; his Bible reading becomes meaningless; rarely, if at all, is his heart touched by any message or special verse. Moreover, his prayer turns dry and dreary as if there is neither sense nor word; and his witnessing appears to be forced and reluctant, not overflowing as before.[74]

Nee likens God's life in us to a river that does not subside, but may cease to flow if hindered by the human flesh.

When God's life stops flowing, one must pray and meditate to find the reason that the Holy Spirit has ebbed in his life. While waiting upon God "he should try to unearth where he has failed to fulfill the condition for the steady flow of God."[75] In every case, the problem is not God but the human flesh.

7) *Deprived of its normal condition, the spirit loses contact with the Holy Spirit and is sometimes darkened.*[75] If the person allows his spirit to be misguided in any way, he may become disconnected from the Holy Spirit and is sometimes darkened.[76] Nee exhorts the believer to keep his spirit in "a tender and pliable state." [77] Otherwise the Christian may come to have a "haughty spirit" (Prov. 16:18) or a spirit that has strayed off the course set by God.

8) "A child of God ought to know what is and what is not the normal condition for his spirit."[78] Nee classifies the spirit according to four conditions:

(a) The spirit is oppressed and is therefore in decline.

(b) The spirit is under compulsion and so is forced into inordinate activity.

(c) The spirit is defiled (2 Corinthians 7:1) since it has yielded ground to sin.

(d) The spirit is quiet and firm because it occupies its rightful position.[78]

It is most important to what Nee calls "the walk of the spirit" that one's spirit be purified from the first three conditions. The spirit in its rightful place enables the flow of God to penetrate to the outward man, so that the work of God may be carried out in His church.

Whenever the laws of the spirit have been obeyed, the spirit reaches a state of "normalcy" and demonstrates certain virtues of the inner man. A normal spirit is humble and contrite (Isa. 57:15), gentle and quiet (1 Pet. 3:4), poor and yet joyful, strong and yet broken, fervent and yet cool. The spirit responds appropriately to the given circumstances. "We must have a spirit of power towards the enemy," Nee says, "a spirit of love towards men, and a spirit of self-control towards ourselves."[80] And in spite of his extensive teaching on the nature of spiritual growth, Nee believes that a normal spirit does not pay a great deal of attention to, or reflection upon, his own spiritual growth. For Nee, "Full salvation delivers a believer out of himself and into God."[81]

In Nee's writings, the human spirit serves as the essential medium between God's presence in the church through the Holy Spirit and man's human presence in the local congregation and the world.[82] Whether the spirit is able to convey what has been communicated or revealed, in large measure, depends upon the function and normalcy of the human soul, the second part of the human triplicity.

The Soul

The soul relates us to ourselves and gives man a sense of reflective awareness, which Nee calls self-consciousness.* While he contends that it is the spirit that God is most concerned with, a greater portion of Nee's anthropological writings is concerned with the nature and operation of the soul. The reason is simple. As has been stated earlier, one of the primary concerns of Nee's ministry was the deliverance of the saints from darkness. The source of that darkness, as Nee interprets it, is the abnormality of the soul within the church.[83] God's desire is to see the soul perfected in its role as the medium through which the spirit can touch the body and thereby enable the spiritual world of revelation to reach the physical world that men communicate and live in. As God seeks to develop further the free functions of the spirit, Satan is active in strengthening the three parts of the human soul—emotion, mind and will—to establish "soulish or carnal Christians" who actively hinder the work of God.

Emotion

"Emotion may be denominated the most formidable enemy to the life of a spiritual Christian," Nee warns.[84] Far too often Christians have allowed their emotions to serve as the barometer of their faith. But the emotional life is one of vacillation and is entirely undependable:

> The emotion of man often displays a reactionary motion: a time of activity in one direction will sometimes produce an opposite reaction. For example, unspeakable sorrow usually follows upon hilarious joy, great depression after high excitement, deep withdrawal after burning fervor. Even in the matter of love, it may commence as such, but due to some emotional alteration, it may end up with a hatred whose intensity far exceeds the earlier love.[85]

Young Christians who have not yet obtained a degree of fitness to receive daily spiritual guidance will invariably turn to their emotions. They are most probably the victims of ignorance and are in need of further teaching and counseling. Others who have walked for some time with Christ, "who have experienced the dividing of spirit and soul and who recognize the stirrings of emotion as being soulish and instantly resist can nonetheless walk after emotion."[86] Their demise is due to the success of some "spiritual" counterfeit by the emotion that outwardly appears to be from the spirit.

For example, one may study psychology as a technique so that his words, teachings, presentations, manners and interpretations can be more psychologically appealing to those whom he wishes to win to Christ.[87] He does not, however, realize that such techniques do not win people to Christ; they only produce psychological conversions that will subside with an alteration of feelings. Such carnality of emotion can only be overcome by exercising the will to submit our emotions to the cross, so that they reflect only the feelings initiated by the spirit.

Affection is an aspect of our emotional life that can hinder the work of the spirit.[88] God demands that we love Him with all our heart, yet the natural man or carnal believer distributes his affection. Love of wife, children, or friends is often set against one's love of God. Yet God desires that we consecrate our affections, so that we will love men—even God—with God's love.[89] Soulish love loves God for the pleasure of the emotion, is interested in the attractions of the world, alternates all too readily, is more active among friends of the opposite sex, and fluctuates broadly according to one's emotions. Contrarily, love in a spiritual man is far above human natural affections and is guided by the spirit.[90]

"Desire occupies the largest part of our emotional life: it joins forces with our will to rebel against God's will."[91] Its influence is greater than mere love of pleasure, for it also includes pride, ambition, inordinate fascination with worldly things, self-justification, and an impetuosity of the flesh that cannot wait upon God. It is God's aim and the experience of the spiritual man that one's desire should be crucified, not suppressed. Once man's desire is that of God's, then the believer finds the rest of a "satisfied life"[92]

The Mind

The mind, the second element of the soul, is extensively described and commented upon in both *The Spiritual Man* and *Spiritual Knowledge*. The latter treatise comes as a shift in Nee's opinion on the nature of the mind. In the former, brain and mind are one; in the latter, a tripartite division is made between the two components and human intuition:

> Now let us further say that man has three different organs for knowledge. In the body is the brain, in the spirit is the intuition, and in the soul is the *nous* [Greek for mind]. When we dissect the brain, we see nothing but the gray and white substance. And intuition is something which we sometimes sense and sometimes do not sense. At times it seems to constrain, at other times it seems to restrain. It is that entity which is deep down in us. But the *nous* stands between the intuition and the brain. It interprets the meaning in the intuition and directs the brain to express it in words.[93]

While the ultimate meaning and interpretation that Nee ascribes to the mind have not shifted, the two books do point to the problem of Nee's attempt to parallel contemporary, postscientific knowledge with the prescientific world view of Scriptures.[94] Regardless of the truth of the Scriptures' human insights, the Bible does not equate or identify brain function with thought.[95] Nee, however, does attempt this, first through a holistic view, equating mind with brain; secondly, with a tripartite division of body (brain), soul (mind), and spirit (intuition).[96]

The mind of the unbeliever is blinded by Satan, corrupted and depraved (Rom. 1:28, 2 Tim. 3:8), futile and vain (Eph. 4:17), fleshly (Col. 2:18) and defiled (Titus 1:15).[97] Whenever the gospel message is presented to him, his mind invents a host of arguments and seasonings to keep himself from seeing the glory of Christ. At this point, a battle rages that will be decided by the exercise of man's will:

Man's will and spirit are like a citadel, which the evil spirits crave to capture. The open field where the battle is waged for the seizure of the citadel is man's mind. Note how Paul the Apostle describes it: "though we live in the world, we are not carrying on a worldy war, for the weapons of our warfare are not worldly, but have divine power to destroy strongholds. We destroy *arguments* and every proud obstacle to the knowledge of God, and take every thought captive to obey Christ" (2 Corinthians 10:3-5). He initially tells of a battle—then where the battle is fought—and finally for what objective. This struggle pertains exclusively to man's mind.[98]

Once man's mind is captured by divine revelation, God's mighty power destroys his agnostic arguments by means of "repentance" (*metanoia* literally means "change of mind").[99]

After regeneration the believer's mind is not liberated totally from Satanic activity and will continue to suffer the onslaught of Satan more than any other organ of the whole man. The mind is his weakest point. Since Satan has lost the first battle upon the believer's conversion, he now concentrates his effort on deceiving the mind with false teachings, prejudices, and narrow-minded theories, opinions and objectives. "History is strewn with innumerable cases of sanctified saints who propagated heresies!" Nee contends.[100] While their hearts* may be in a state of active communication with God, they may unknowingly accept Satanic suggestions. Such believers, who have not had their minds renewed in their Christian walk, show their lack of common sense and practical wisdom by their outward actions. Neglecting the proper use of their minds, their thoughts are cluttered with a collage of diverse thoughts and worldly images.

---

* Nee defines "heart" as the "conscience" and the "mind." The heart acts as an exchange between the workings of the Spirit and soul: "The spirit reaches the soul via the heart; and through the heart the soul conveys to the spirit what it has gathered from outside."[101]

Many other mental symptoms can be attributed to the work of the enemy and can be quite easily distinguished from spiritual insights. Unlike "normal" mental activity, abnormal thoughts from Satan always appear without any conscious effort of the will.[102] The operating requirements of the Holy Spirit and of the evil spirit in the brain are also different:

(1) All supernatural revelations, visions, or other strange occurrences which require total cessation of the function of the mind, or are obtained only after it has ceased working, are not of God.

(2) All visions, which arise from the Holy Spirit, are conferred when the believer's mind is fully active. It necessitates the active engagement of the various functions of the mind to apprehend these visions. The endeavors of evil spirits follow exactly the opposite course.

(3) All which flows from God agrees with God's nature and the Bible.[103]

Once a person is aware of this, he should exercise his will, and resist the enemy with the power of Christ.

All too often, the believer has let his mind be overrun with evil by giving ground to Satan in six different ways: (1) through an unrenewed mind that has not been consecrated to God; (2) through a mind that cherishes sin; (3) by misunderstanding God's truth and accepting a lie; (4) by accepting satanic suggestions, particularly in discerning his circumstances and the future; (5) by allowing the mind to be blank and atrophied, out of a lack of proper mental experiences; and (6) by prayer done with a passive mind.[104]

Nee is particularly critical of popular philosophies and theologies that encourage a passivity of mind. Scientific hypnotism, yoga, and even many teachings on the reception of the gift of tongues[105] instruct adherents to let their minds go free or become blank, and Nee believes this to be unbiblical. "By examining every instance in the New Testament where God's supernatural revelation is recounted," Nee states, "we find that everyone there who experiences a revelation does so with his mind functioning and with the ability to *control himself* and use any part of his body."[106] Many intellectual and psychological works of Satan, including false teachings, insomnia, forgetfulness, mental fatigue, theological vacillation, talkativeness, and obstinacy, have entered into the life of the church and the life of the believer through a passive mind.

Once the mind has been renewed through the work of the cross, it acts as an auxiliary to the human spirit.[107] Whenever the spirit, for whatever reason, is not led to pray or does not deliver some needed guidance from the Holy Spirit, the mind exercises its understanding by actively praying. This is, at least, Nee's interpretation of "pray[ing] with the mind" in 1 Corinthians 14:15.[108] In so doing, the mind of the soul is within the proper organismic relationship as a steward of the spirit.[109] Likewise the spirit receives knowledge intuitively, but needs our mental faculties to understand its meaning. The mind also serves as the translator of truth received through the preaching of the Word by other members of the body of Christ. Finally, the mind is most able to serve the spirit when it is exercised in the systematic reading and memorization of God's Word.

The Will

According to God's plan in the Christian life, the will, the third and final component of Nee's tripartite soul, ought to be in submission to the will of God.[110] Whether the will is in submission depends not upon an unconditional predetermination of God's elect, but rather upon the decision of "the sovereign, independent, free will of man."[111]* Nee clearly differs from the rigid "five-point" Calvinistic perspective, in that he affirms a universal atonement and that man's will plays an important part in the regenerative/ sanctification process of the Christian life.

Still Nee does see the prodigious damage suffered by the human volition/will as a result of the fall. In the Garden of Eden, placed between the two massive contradictory wills of God and Satan, man chose to ignore the will of the Creator for the created, and his own will became captive and underwent corruption.[113] Without God' intervention in history all of mankind would remain fleshly, unable to save himself, perform any spiritual good, or avoid sinning. On two different occasions, Nee has compared John 1:13 and Rev. 22:17 and concluded that the only way to reconcile the two texts is to insist that the will is effectual unto salvation only because salvation commences with God. The will cannot save itself; it can only accept or reject God's salvation gift of love toward him in the form of Jesus Christ.[114]

The importance of the will in carrying out God's purposes in man's life does not end with salvation. Every step of the Christian walk requires a surrender of our own wills and an absolute yielding to God's will. Many of God's children, Nee warns, will go through "various unpleasant strippings" in order that our wills may be proven faithful:

> He causes them to lose material things: health, fame, position, usefulness. What is more, He even causes them

---

* Nee goes on to say, "Though God is the Lord of the entire universe, yet He is willing to be restricted by a non-encroachment of man's free will. He never forces man to be loyal to Him. And Satan likewise is unable to usurp any part of man without the latter's consent granted either knowingly or unknowingly. Both God and the devil require man to be persuaded before operating in him. When man 'desires' good, God will accomplish it; but when he 'desires' evil, the wicked spirit will fulfill it. This is what we see in the Garden of Eden."[116]

to be deprived of joyous feeling, burning desire, the presence and comfort of God. He must show them that everything except His will must be denied. If it is God's will, they should be willing to accept pain and suffering upon their physical bodies. They must be ready to embrace dryness, darkness, and coldness if He seems pleased to so treat them. Even if He should so strip them of everything, of even so called spiritual effectiveness, they must accept it. He wishes His own to know that He saves them not for their enjoyment but for His Own will. In gain or loss, joy or sorrow, consciousness of His presence or that of His rejection, Christians must contemplate God's will alone.[115]

According to Nee, the intent of God here is twofold: He desires, first, that our wills obey Him and, secondly, that the "tendency" or "life" of the will that secretly awaits the opportunity to disobey be "smashed," broken, and put to death. Through the working of the cross, the believer will be both in obedience and in harmony with the universal will of God.

There are two dangerous attitudes which the believer must be aware of, so that he will not give ground in his will to evil spirits. Nee classifies these dangers as one of commission and one of omission; positive sins and negative sins:

> Positive sins are those which a person commits: his hands perform bad acts, his eyes see evil scenes, his ears hear wicked voices, and his mouth speaks unclean words. These render opportunity to evil spirits in varying degree to take hold of the hands, eyes, ears and mouth of the saint.[116]

Such actions of willful sinning are the enemy's strategy among the "heathen" and among carnal Christians. Among Christians desirous of growing in grace, deception is offered in the way of negation or passivity of the will. Nee quotes Jessie Penn-Lewis and defines passivity as "a cessation of the active exercise of the will in control over spirit, soul and body, or either, as may be the case."[116]

Passive-willed Christians falsely believe that only God will energize their works and that nothing will be done apart from God's will and plan. Yet, inactivity of the will only leads to inactivity of action. Such people wait for some external force to move them. These external motivations usually arise from the "prince of this world" and enable Satan to use our God-given talents and charismatic gifts according to his will and plan. Eventually these people become entrenched in a life that feels happy only when it is forced to do something.[118]

The source of the problem is ignorance, experienced even by spiritual brethren. While their motive in seeking God's will in their lives may be entirely pure and spiritual, they do not understand that God does not want man to be ordered mechanically and unconsciously.[119] In their false rationality, they consider themselves beyond deception because of their frequent spiritual experiences. In addition, they no longer understand the means of keeping their minds open to knowledge received in the Bible, by watching and praying.

Passive wills may be the result of personal laziness, but most often, they are the results of misunderstanding the content of Scripture. Some misconstrue Gal. 2:20 to connote spiritual life as a life of self-effacement, achieved through a loss of personality and an absence of volition and self-control, and demonstrated in automatic obedience to God.[120] Others view Phil. 2:13 as denying the need for our own readiness "To will and to work." Many other misconceptions arise, particularly out of ignorance of the work of the spirit in obedience (Acts 5:32), the ruling of our spirit, speaking (Matt. 10:20), guidance (Isa. 30:21), memory (John 14:26), love (Rom. 5:5), weakness and suffering (2 Cor. 12:10), and humility (2 Cor. 10:12ff.).[121] In every case Christians have assumed that these matters may be best governed by a passive will that unquestionably accepts whatever occurs to them.

Obviously, the way of recovery from the negative and positive sins of the will is through the exercise of the human will according to the Scriptures. First, Nee says, we must obey God's will through our own willingness and through openness to His revelation and strengthening. Secondly, we must resist the devil's will with all the strength of our spirit, soul, and body.* Finally, one must resolve to follow

God's pathway to freedom through the further exercising of the human will in collaboration with the collective will of the saints.[123]

The Soul: Its Latent Power

"Today's situation is perilous," wrote Nee in 1933.[124] As his indigenous movement began to grow and spread through China, he became increasingly aware of what he regarded as counterfeit spirituality within and without the Christian church. Healings, tongues,† miracles, prophecy, and meditation, he believed, were all being satanically manifested to mislead those who sought the truth and power of God.[126] Within the framework of his tripartite anthropology, he propounded a vaccine and a remedy in the dividing and discerning of the power of the Spirit emanating from the human spirit and the latent power originating with the soul.[127]

While the power in man's soul was at one time intended to serve God, it has now been outlawed as an energy source

---

* The resistance of the saints, however, must include the acceptance of our mistakes. "The worst fallacy one can ever commit is to reckon oneself infallible."[122]

† Animistic practices in Nee's Fukien Province included the practice of spirit possession by a young medium or "tang-ki." In these possessions the medium shakes and "performs unintelligible 'gods' language."[125]

unfit for the body of Christ.[1][2857] The tremendous soul power exercised by Adam to name and rule the earth has been subjugated and circumscribed by the flesh as a result of the fall. Originally in the "likeness" of God's power, it can easily manufacture gifts quite like those "of the Spirit." Such supernaturalism can even be produced by Christians if Satan sufficiently tempts them to labor, even for the church, independently of God. If, for example, prayer is projected towards the sick person instead of towards God, that person will become oppressed by the psychic/soulical power and will become even sicker. Others may use hypnotic techniques, singing, and novel Bible teaching to bring about certain results, but in every case the real fruit of the spiritual life will be altogether absent. Christians in such instances have preferred the supernatural things of the psychic world rather than the supranatural working of God within the church. Rarely do readers of the Bible, in Chinese, English, or Hebrew, find the latent power of the soul in the story of Adam. Nee probably would not have seen it without the help of G. H. Pember's *The Earth's Earliest Age.*

Nee criticizes non-Christian religions for practicing aesthetic principles that release the power of the soul through overcoming the flesh. Whenever such goals are carried out, supernatural powers become available, including healings, mind reading, predicting the future, and piercing the unknown past. Quite deceptively, Satan, through these cults and religions, causes men to substitute God's salvation and life for psychic miracles; what is of the spirit for what is of the soul.

The Body

In *The Spiritual Man*, Watchman Nee's study on the human body is much briefer and less complex than his analysis of

---

[57] As in the example of Jesus' life.

G. H. Pember's Era

High Miller, a Christian turned amateur scientist, discovered that rock sediments indicated an earth older than six thousand years. Thomas Chalmers, another Christian studying science, lectured on the enormity of the universe. Dinosaurs, extinct animals, were appearing in exhibitions at the British Museum. Believers had always thought it safe to ply the Heavens and the earth for evidence of the Divine, merciful Creator. But the sciences, natural philosophy, appeared to differ with Biblical theology.

The Victorian era was also an era of doubt. People turned their backs on the power of God and looked to the power of steam and great engines for a new tower of Babylon. For hope in eternal life, they went back to the pagan traditions of spirit mediums. The spiritualists taught that at death, the person's spirit survives, leaves the body, and wants to speak to the living. Victor Hugo tried to contact his beloved daughter. Mary Todd Lincoln went to séances to contact her son and later dead husband Abraham. At these séances "the dead" spoke through mediums. There is no judgment. Christian editorials warned believers that the disembodied voices they heard at séances were really demons.

In defense of the Christian faith, G. H. Pember proposed his own unified theory to explain in one book geological evidence, the majestic heavens, and spiritism. Pember's ideas in *The Earth's Earliest Age* were good for the evidence available in the nineteenth century. In the twentieth century, magicians such as Harry Houdini and James Randi showed that psychics and spiritualists can do tricks. Both men searched for genuine phenomena. It is not so much powerful, demonic spirits as a lying spirits.

the soul and the spirit. The reason is simple. The physician and biologist use their physical senses, aided by scientific instruments, to observe and describe the functions and structure of the physical body. The soul and spirit are metaphysical elements and beyond natural observation. Nee was neither a doctor nor a biologist and therefore did not attempt to write any "tripartite" description of the body, according to a series of interacting units, as he had done with spirit and the soul. The local churches had invested him with the job of metaphysician, and, using the historic tools of the "inspired" Scripture in conjunction with personal revelation, Nee felt confident enough in the position to propose a practical metaphysical map of the soul and the spirit. Conversely, the body was the realm of the physician. Nee did, however, remark on such physical matters that pertain to spiritual life.

Using Rom. 8:11 as a text, Nee taught that the believer can have life in his mortal body prior to the resurrection of the dead.* In this life the nature of the body is not unchangeable, for the quality of the body can be quickened, as evident in two ways: "(1) He will restore us when we are sick and (2) He will preserve us if we are not sick."[130] In the first, God heals us so that the spiritual work of the church may not be hindered by any sickness. In the second, the body is preserved from the assault of any disease or infirmity in order that it may perform services within the larger body of Christ. While accepting the use of modern medical aids when justified,[130] Nee stressed that the believer also has the spiritual potential to overcome the forces of sickness that seek to hinder the work of God.

The essential requirement for the believer to have this "life" in his body is to live the obedient life of the spiritual

---

* It is most likely that Paul is here referring to the final resurrection of the body, contra. Nee. See n. 129.

man. The spiritual man acknowledges his inability to control
his own health. He allows the Holy Spirit to make real the
crucifixion of the deeds and sicknesses of the body:

> Only the Holy Spirit can take what the cross has
> accomplished and make the believers experience it. If we
> hear the truth of the cross but do not allow Him to work into
> our lives, then we know nothing but a theory and an ideal.[132]

Nee uses 1 Corinthians 6:12-40, with its emphasis on
the human body as members in the body of Christ, to
support his belief that God desires the full deliverance of
the body from fleshly needs, sin, and physical ills. Through
the medium of the Spirit, we are healed by His stripes.[133]
Under the governorship of the same Spirit, the body of the
spiritual man responds to its natural needs only insofar as
it glorifies the Lord, not for the satisfaction of personal
desires. Likewise, to sin against the body is to sin against
Christ, for the body is God's temple.[134] In all, surrender to
the work of the Holy Spirit is a necessary condition—the
essence—of the spiritual man.

In the matter of sickness, Nee gives extended comments
upon the relationship between sin and sickness and between
sickness and sanctification.[135] Sin is closely correlated with
sickness in the life of the believer. Not in a negative sense—
where sickness is regarded as punishment for unconfessed
wickedness and vice—but in a positive way sickness is
interpreted as an important opportunity for the faithful to
perceive whether his life is centered on the self or upon the
witness of the spirit:

> The heart of a believer is far from God's. God permits
> him to be ill that he may forget himself; but the more ill he
> grows the more self-loving he becomes; he endlessly dwells
> on his symptoms in his anxiety to find a cure. Almost all
> thoughts revolve about himself! How attentive he now is
> to his food, what he should or should not eat!

How worried he is when anything goes awry! He takes great care for his comforts and rest. He agonizes if he feels a bit hot or cold or has suffered a bad night, as though these were fatal to his life. How sensitive he is to the way people treat him: do they think enough of him, do they take good care of him, do they visit him as often as they should? Countless hours are exhausted in just this way of thinking about his body; and so he has no time to meditate on the Lord or on what the Lord may be wanting to accomplish in his life. Indeed, many are simply "bewitched" by their sickness! We never truly know how excessively much we love ourselves until we become sick![136]

Sickness is the result of the universal fall of man and therefore is a universal condition. No man, Christian or non-Christian alike, experiences perpetually perfect health. But individually, the believer must ask what is the reason for the sickness that has befallen him. Patiently, the Christian should find God's purpose in allowing infirmity to fall upon him. Has some transgression gone unnoticed; has he defiled his body—the temple of God—or; more likely, is God further instructing him to deny self and to trust God and His spirit? Once the ill believer has settled this question, he can begin to recover. Trusting in God, he will no longer covet a cure through man's drugs, but will abide by the spirit's leading. Recovery is inevitable according to the physical (medical) and spiritual means provided for by God. Only when "a Christian plainly knows his work is finished"[137] will the sickness end in death. Until that time death must be resisted by our abiding faith in the work of the cross.[138]

The Fourfold Work of the Cross

How does one appropriate the work of Christ? This question provides much of the conflict and dynamics of the extensive writings of Watchman Nee. Yet, studies done by Erling, Kinnear, Henry, and Lyall[139] have entirely ignored or seem unaware of this, the major input of his teachings. In

The Spiritual Man and *The Normal Christian Life* the question
of redemptive appropriation is presented in the form of a
fourfold work of the cross upon the personhood and labors
of the believer. Each of these phases of the cross has a specific
pattern of revelation and then experience. Further, the
experience "usually takes the two-fold form of a crisis leading
to a continuous process."[140] The end result of this process is
the spiritual man. And the ongoing life of the spiritual man
is the normal Christian life.

The first two works of grace are concerned with the
state of our being. The next two are concerned with the
nature of our service. The order here of resolving the
problems of being before the patterns of service are fashioned
is most important. For all true service begins with the
regenerated person whose soul submits to the spirit's
intuition, communion, and conscience and not with the
unregenerate man whose soul rebels and succumbs to the
passions of the body. All that an unregenerated person is,
according to Nee, is "flesh." And once this flesh has been
dealt with, the believer can walk in the spirit and stand before
the foe, to the service and glory of God, by the strength
received in the last two works of grace.[141]

Justification

The first work of grace is, most obviously, "justification and
the new birth."[142] Our individual sinfulness and the Lord's
work on the cross must first be inwardly and preveniently
revealed to the unregenerate. Thereupon he has the
opportunity either to reject the gospel or to experience
repentance and the initial faith in Christ. In the latter, he
becomes a new creation and continues to live a life of
maintained fellowship with God (process).

Much of what Nee says about this first step is neither
new nor distinctive of his theology. Other Christians have

written that in salvation the blood deals with a person's sins and is primarily for God; the cross is for the sinner and procures deliverance from the old man; and through Christ's substitutionary death, the believer proceeds from death into eternal life.[143] But in Nee regeneration is also a phenomenon of the human spirit. In *The Spiritual Man* he writes:

> Man's spirit needs to be quickened because it is born dead. The new birth, which the Lord spoke to Nicodemus, is the new birth of the spirit. It certainly is not a physical birth as Nicodemus suspected, nor is it a soulical one. We must note carefully that the new birth imparts God's life to the spirit of man. Inasmuch as Christ has atoned for our soul and destroyed the principle of the flesh, so we who are joined to Him participate in His resurrection life. We have been united with Him in His death; consequently, it is in our spirit that we first reap the realization of His resurrection life. New birth is something, which happens entirely within the spirit; it has no relation to soul or body.[144]

Again in *The Normal Christian Life*, this premise serves as the structural base to his understanding of the Christian walk. While this teaching is not specifically stated here, Nee does quote Ezek. 36:26 as evidence that conversion is an act of the heart and of a new spirit, not a purification of the flesh.[145]

Likewise in both *The Spiritual Man* and *The Normal Christian Life*, Nee envisions a conflict raging between a life according to the intuitive witness of the spirit and one according to the workings of the soul and the desires of the flesh.[146] Accordingly, this conflict cannot be realized in the individual unless his spirit has been quickened/made alive in conversion.

Deliverance from Sin

In the first work of grace, man has become conscious that Jesus died for his sins upon the cross. In the second work of grace, he becomes aware that he himself shares Christ's death.

It is by grace that man is forgiven of his sins and is justified in God's sight, and it is also by God's grace that man is delivered from his own propensity to violate God's laws. It is this second work of grace that Nee calls "deliverance from sin."

Nee acknowledges that "this liberation from this power of sin ... may be experienced the very hour a sinner accepts the Lord Jesus as Savior and is born anew."[147] Yet many more undergo a time of despair in their attempt to live a life worthy of God's calling. When one appropriates the blood of Christ that has dealt with our sins, Nee teaches, a civil war ensues in our hearts. For now, our spirits daily strive against the life of the soul and its sin principle.

In the cross of Christ, the sin principle is dealt with. Like justification and the new birth, deliverance from sin begins when a man realizes his utter sinfulness. He must see that justification has not eradicated the sin principle. In prayer at the foot of the cross, the believer learns an important lesson in the Christian life: " ... knowing this, that our old man was crucified with Him, that the body of sin might be done away, so that we should no longer be in bondage to sin."[148] By the revelation of God's Word, we "know" that the crucifixion of the old man is an accomplished fact in God's eyes.

Experientially the believer responds in the crisis of his crucifixion and in the process of his resurrection. Paul exhorts the believer, "Reckon ye also yourselves to be dead unto sin, but alive unto God."[149] First the believer's old man, that is, his flesh, must be crucified. In this relinquishing of the life of the old man to the work of the cross, sin itself will no longer have dominion over the body.

Nowhere, Nee cautions, does the Scripture say that the root of sin within is eradicated, nor does God require man to suppress the body without (asceticism).[150] Until the glorification of our bodies, the Christian can only sustain a life delivered from sin through the process of continual consecration.[151]

Nee's key texts for understanding consecration are Rom. 6:13, 16, 19, and 12:1-3.[152] On the basis of these texts, Nee sees consecration as first an activity of the will, the third element of the soul, seeking to abide in Him.[153] Secondly, consecration involves a co-resurrection with Christ, whereby the source of the Christian's life is God himself.[154] And thirdly, consecration's aim is to wait on God to serve Him.[155] Once the will has been so consecrated, the believer is "fully occupied with the divinity as well as the humanity of the Lord, with the divine strength and the unleavened life of the Lord, with the Holy Spirit, and with the Lord's sensitivity."[156]

Prior to the believer's deliverance, the body sinned as a consequence of the old man. Once delivered, the old man is reckoned as crucified, to the end that sin no longer has dominion over the body.

The first two works of grace have thus far quickened our spirits in salvation and freed our bodies from the power of sin. As yet, the soul's nature has been unaffected.

Much of what these first two works of grace have done is remedial—undoing the damage done in man's fall in the Garden of Eden. The final two works are not remedial, but are positive, in the direction of serving God's eternal purposes.[157] According to Nee, these purposes can best be comprehended through an analysis of God's commands in the Garden of Eden.[158] God commanded Adam to eat from every tree except the tree of the knowledge of good and evil. The problem with this tree is that while man would no longer be ethically ignorant, he would also no longer be dependent upon God for his moral choice.

God did desire that he should partake freely of the fruit of the tree of life. And how does Nee perceive the meaning of this tree of life? It is God himself.

... for God is life. He is the highest form of life, and He is also the source and goal of life. And the fruit: what is that? It is our Lord Jesus Christ. You cannot eat the tree but you can eat the fruit. No one is able to receive God as God, but we can receive the Lord Jesus.[159]

Grace is therefore given so that the believer may more and more freely partake of the life-giving tree.

The Gift of the Holy Spirit

Much controversy has arisen in the contemporary church concerning the reception and evidence of the Pentecostal experience described in the second chapter of the Book of Acts. The same was true in China during the period of Watchman Nee's active ministry.[160] His own position is unlike that of traditional Pentecostal or modern charismatic theology.[161] Nee believes that the Spirit comes not through tarrying but through revelation. And that revelation is of Christ exalted upon His throne.[162] Thus the key text for realizing the Spirit outpoured is not Acts 1:4 but Peter's statement in 2:33-36. Once this is acknowledged by faith, then the crisis experience comes as the "Spirit outpoured"

The nature of the crisis experience, Nee emphasizes, is quite diverse. Citing the experiences of R.A. Torrey, Dwight L. Moody, and Charles G. Finney,[163] Nee concludes that "we must leave God free to work as He wills" and "that each one whom the Spirit of God falls [sic] will unfailingly know it."[164]

The continued process is the Spirit indwelling, which is the very person of Jesus living in us. The Holy Spirit then provides us with the potential power to live the victorious life. But since it is Christ in us, that victory is only ours if we have "reverence" for Him and consciously recognize His presence.[165]

This idea of reverence for the exalted Christ permits Nee to speak of all Christians as having the Holy Spirit, but not all having the Spirit outpoured/indwelling experience. This gift of the Holy Spirit experienced in a later working of the cross is one requiring a revelation of the fact of that indwelling at conversion. It is only then that the Spirit can begin to revolutionize the life of the believer.[166]

At this point in the believer's life, the Spirit indwelling within the human spirit is more and more making His presence felt in the human soul. But in order that the body may completely manifest the Spirit's bidding and be pleasing to God, the Christian must again receive further revelation from God.

Pleasing God

The fourth and final aspect of grace in the life of the believer is the most extensively written phase in Nee's writings. About half of *The Normal Christian Life* deals with this issue, and a majority of Nee's writings deal in some way with the practical aspect of "pleasing God."

Nee begins his discussion with an analysis of the meaning and value of Romans 7.[167] How does the Christian respond to the Old Testament law? The law is scriptural, and yet by trying to obey the law, we are in essence denying the all-sufficiency of Christ. Nee understands the key to understanding Romans 7 is in Romans 7:18-19:

> For I know that in me, that is, in my flesh, dwelleth no good thing: for to will is present with me, but to do that which is good is not. For the good which I would I do not: but the evil which I would not, that I practice.[168]

In these verses is a summary of the purpose of the law and an important insight into the nature of the believer's service to God. The law sets for us a standard of what is good. But as Paul has stated in verse 19, the good is unattainable. For the law was written to show us that we cannot serve or do something for God. Using Paul's analogy in 7:1-4, only death can separate us from the law with its impossible requirements. Only then can we be united with Christ, the new husband, "who with every demand He makes becomes in ... [us] the power for its fulfillment."[169] In order for us to fulfill the law, we must put to death "the flesh," our "will" and our "doing." The revelation therefore for "pleasing God" is not an effort at trying to succeed in some established ethics or missionary goals but God's requirement for us to "cease from doing" through seeing the work of the cross. We are to stop trying to do God's will through our own will power, because such efforts are "soulical." For the only work of the church is one of justification and sanctification "through Jesus Christ our Lord" (7:25).

The continuing process of "pleasing God," to walk according to the Spirit (Rom. 8:4), is a task that constantly engages the faith of the spiritual man. His life is one of more and more of the Spirit enhancing, educating, and refining himself by daily bearing the cross upon the soul life, to the end that he can declare with Paul, "It is no longer I, but Christ in me."[170]

"The finished work of the cross," Nee writes, "and its continual application by the Holy Spirit are consequently inseparable."[171] Within Nee's trichotomy, the Holy Spirit dwells within the human spirit. But in order for there to be a release of the Spirit, the soul must yield to the cross, just as the flesh yielded in justification. Our feelings must be crucified, for they by themselves will hinder God's work.[172] Our mind must be renewed through the work of the cross.[173] The will must also actively surrender itself at the foot of the cross to be preserved from Satan's lies.[174] The cross even brings victory over the power of physical death.[175]

In *The Release of the Spirit*, Nee succinctly presents the meaning of the work of the cross upon the soul and its affect upon our spirit:

> When we really understand the cross we shall see it means the breaking of the outward man viz., [the soul]. The cross reduces the outward man to death; it splits open the human shell. The cross must destroy all that belongs to our outward man—our opinions, our ways, our cleverness, our self-love, our all. The way is clear, in fact, crystal clear.
>
> As soon as our outward man is destroyed, our spirit can easily come forth.[176]

When the spirit, the agent and vehicle of the Holy Spirit in the church, is in a state of constant release as the cross works upon the soul, the body will do the work of God, and the believer will be as a spiritual man.

In understanding this principle it is possible to understand the extensive and meticulous attention that Nee's writings give on such matters as Bible study,[177] preaching,[178] prayer,[179] sleeping,[180] marriage,[181] family life,[182] witnessing,[183] separation from the world,[184] finance,[185] clothing and eating,[186] and the church's life itself [187] through a highly allegorical method of exegesis. While a majority of Christian authors present certain biblical guidelines on such matters, Nee is concerned to present them in the light of his perception of what is "soulical" and what is spiritual. For the "soulical" man labors in vain, but the spiritual builds upon Christ, the true foundation.

Now there is a secret for understanding Watchman Nee's ideas about the Spiritual man. Read the preceding section and substitute we/us every time you find the words spirit, soul, and body.

Chapter 4 Endnotes

1. C. Ryder Smith, *The Biblical Doctrine of Man* (London: The Epworth Press, 1951), passim.

2. Nee, *Spiritual Man*, 1:7.

3. Tertullian's *De Anima* is dichotomous. Origen's *De Principiis* supports a trichotomy.

4. See Warfield, *Perfectionism*, pp. 216-311.

5. See Jean Marc Etienne Cruvellier, *L'Exégèse de Romains 7 et Le Mouvement de Keswick* (S-Gravenhage: Vrije Universiteit to Amsterdam, 1961).

6. Rev. J.B. Heard, *The Tripartite Nature of Man* (Edinburgh: T. & T. Clark, 1875). Mary E. McDonough, *God's Plan of Redemption* (Boston: Hamilton Brothers, 1922). Andrew Murray, *The Spirit of Christ* (Fort Washington, Pa.: Christian Literature Crusade, 1963). G.H. Pember, *Earth's Earliest Ages* (Old Tappan, N.J.: Fleming H. Revell Company, n.d.). Jessie Penn-Lewis, *Soul and Spirit: A Glimpse into Bible Psychology* (Dorset, England: The Overcomer Literature Trust, n.d.). Delavan Leonard Pierson, *Arthur T. Pierson* (New York: Fleming H. Revell Company, 1912), p. 283.

7. Nee, *Spiritual Man*, 1:21-22.

8. Ibid., 1:22.

9. Ibid., p. 23; idem, *The Release of the Spirit* (Indianapolis: Premium Literature Co., 1965), p. 29.

10. Heard, *Tripartite Nature*, pp. 39-49; McDonough, *Plan*, pp. 21-22; Pember, *Ages*, pp. 103-16; Penn-Lewis, *Soul*, p. 4; Rev. C.I. Scofield, gen. ed., *The Scofield Reference Bible*, 2nd ed. (New York: Oxford University Press, 1917), loc. cit. (A. T. Pierson is listed here as a consulting editor).

11. Nee, *Spiritual Man*, 1:23-26; idem, *Latent Power*, pp. 10-11; idem, *Christian Life*, pp. 155-56.

12. Idem, *Spiritual Man*, 1:24; cf. *Knowledge*, p. 85.

13. Ibid., pp. 26-28.

14. Ibid., p. 26.

15. exM/exMthen: Matt. 23:27,28; 2 Corinthians 4:16; 1 Per. 3:3. esM/esMthen: Luke 11:39; Rom. 7:22; Eph. 3:16.

16. Taken from McDonough, *Plan*, p. viii.

17. Nee, *Latent Power*, p. 15.

18. Idem, *Spiritual Man*, 1:44; 3:158.

19. Ibid., 1:43.

20. Idem, *Christian Life*, p. 80.

21. Ibid., p. 81.

22. Idem, *Spiritual Man*, 1:46.

23. Ibid., p. 47.

24. Ibid., p. 50.

25. Idem, *Christian Life*, pp. 110-11.

26. Nee, *Spiritual Man*, 1:31-41.

27. See Nee, *Spiritual Man*, 1:35.

28. Ibid., p. 34.

29. Ibid., pp. 7-20.

30. Ibid., pp. 29-30.

31. Ibid., p. 55.

32. Ibid., pp. 57-60.

33. William L. Lane, *The Gospel According to Mark: The English Text with Introduction, Exposition and Notes, The New International Commentary* on the New Testament (Grand Rapids: William B. Eerdmans Publishing Company, 1974), p. 564.

34. Nee, *Spiritual Man*, 1:60; idem, *Christian Life*, passim; idem, *Living Sacrifice*, pp. 14-17; idem, *Not I, But Christ*, pp. 114-20; idem, *Gospel Dialogue* (New York: Christian Fellowship Publishers, 1975), pp. 67, 98.

35. Andrew Murray, *The Spirit of Christ*, pp. 14-16; Nee, *Not I, But*

Christ, p. 132.

36. Nee, *Christian Life*, pp. 141-44.

37. Idem, *Christ the Sum*, p. 59.

38. Ibid.

39. Idem, *Spiritual Man*, 2:10-14.

40. Ibid., 2:10.

41. Ibid., p. 26.

42. Ibid., pp. 67-70.

43. Ibid., p. 69.

44. Nee, *Spiritual Man*, 2:70.

45. 1 John 2:20, 27 RSV; Nee, *Spiritual Man*, 2:73.

46. Ibid., p. 75.

47. Ibid., pp. 57-76.

48. Ibid., p. 77.

49. See pp. 65ff.

50. Nee, *Spiritual Man*, 2:77.

51. Ibid., p. 78.

52. Ibid., p. 80.

53. Ibid.

54. Ibid., p. 88.

55. Ibid., pp. 52-55, 58.

56. Idem, *Prayer Ministry*, p. 17.

57. Idem, *Spiritual Man*, 2:107.

58. Ibid., p. 111.

59. Ibid., p. 118.

60. Ibid., p. 123. Cf. John Wesley, *Wesley's Standard Sermons*, 2 vols., ed. Edward H. Sugden (Nashville: Lamar & Barton, n.d.),

1:121; idem, *The Works of John Wesley*, 14 vols., ed. Thomas Jackson, reprint ed. (Kansas City, Mo.: Nazarene Publishing House, n.d.), 10: 394-406.

61. Nee, *Spiritual Man*, 2:122-25.

62. Ibid., p. 68.

63. Ibid., pp. 145-46.

64. Ibid., p. 146.

65. Ibid., pp. 146-48.

66. Ibid., pp. 148-50.

67. Ibid., p. 150.

68. Ibid.

69. Ibid., pp. 151-53.

70. Ibid., p. 151.

71. Lee, *Nee*, p. 137.

72. Ibid., 3:153-56.

73. Ibid., 2:156-58.

74. Ibid., pp. 156-157.

75. Ibid.

76. Ibid., pp. 158-60.

77. Ibid., p. 160.

78. Ibid.

79. Ibid.

80. Ibid., p. 180.

81. Ibid., p. 176.

82. Ibid., 1:26; idem, *Release*, pp. 10-12; *Knowledge*, p. 85. Here the relationship is most explicitly stated.

83. Nee, *Spiritual Man*, 1:144-78; *Latent Power*, pp. 32-36, 45-56, 64-80; *Christian Life*, pp. 158-63; *Spiritual Reality*, pp. 10-64.

84. Idem, *Spiritual Man*, 2:191.

85. Ibid., p. 190.

86. Ibid., p. 194.

87. Ibid., p. 196.

88. Ibid., pp. 202-11; *Christian Life*, p. 174.

89. Nee, *Spiritual Man*, 2:202.

90. Ibid., p. 211.

91. Ibid., p. 212.

92. Ibid., p. 222.

93. Idem, *Knowledge*, p. 91.

94. For an understanding of the prescientific, mythopoetic mind of the Bible writers, see H. and H.A. Frankfort, John H. Wilson and Thorkild Jacobsen, *Before Philosophy: The Intellectual Adventure of Ancient Man* (Baltimore: Penguin Books, 1951), pp. 137-234.

95. Heard, *Tripartite Nature*, p. 52.

96. Nee, *Spiritual Man*, 3:7.

97. Ibid., 3:8.

98. Ibid., pp. 7-8.

99. Ibid., pp. 9-10.

100. Ibid., p. 12.

101. Idem, *Knowledge*, p. 86.

102. Idem, *Spiritual Man*, 3:14.

103. Ibid., p. 27.

104. Ibid., pp. 18-27.

105. Ibid., p. 28.

106. Ibid.

107. Idem, *Knowledge*, pp. 119ff.

108. Idem, *Spiritual Man*, 3:163-70.

109. See p. 79ff.

110. Idem, *Dialogue*, pp. 106-8; idem, *Spiritual Man*, 2:75-77.

111. Idem, *Spiritual Man*, 3:77.

112. Ibid., p. 95.

113. Ibid., p. 78.

114. Ibid., pp. 78-79; idem, *Dialogue*, pp. 106-7.

115. Idem, *Spiritual Man*, 3:85.

116. Ibid., pp. 91-92.

117. Penn-Lewis and Evans, *War*, pp. 69-70, quoted in Nee, *Spiritual Man*, 3:93.

118. Nee, *Spiritual Man* 3:98.

119. Ibid., p. 97.

120. Ibid., pp. 104-7.

121. Ibid., pp. 109-18.

122. Ibid., p. 123.

123. Ibid., pp. 125-36.

124. Idem, *Latent Power*, p. 8.

125. David K. Jordon, Gods, *Ghosts, and Ancestors: The Folk Religion of a Taiwanese Village* (Los Angeles: University of California Press, 1972), p. 74.

126. Nee, *Latent Power*, pp. 32ff.

127. Idem, *Release*, pp. 66-67.

128. Idem, *Latent Power*, pp. 85-86.

129. John Murray, *The Epistle to the Romans*, The New International Commentary on the New Testament (Grand Rapids: William B. Eerdmans Publishing Company, 1965), p. 292.

130. Nee, *Spiritual Man*, 3:143.

131. See ibid., pp. 168-73.

132. Ibid., pp. 148ff.

133. Ibid., pp. 183-84; cf. Isa. 53:4-5.

134. Nee, *Spiritual Man*, 3:161ff.

135. Ibid., pp. 158-95.

136. Ibid., pp. 166-67.

137. Ibid., p. 218.

138. Ibid.

139. Bernard Erling, "The Story of Watchman Nee," *Lutheran Quarterly* 28 (May 1976):140-55. Kinnear, *Against the Tide*. Carl F.H. Henry, "Footnotes: Watchman Nee," *Christianity Today*, May 9, 1975, pp. 31-32. Lyall, *Mighty Men*.

140. Nee, *Christian Life*, p. 141.

141. Idem, *Sit*, passim.

142. Idem, *Christian Life*, pp. 9-22; *Living Sacrifice*, pp. 3-14; *Spiritual Man* 1:55-82.

143. E.g., Leon Morris, *The Apostolic Preaching of the Cross* (Grand Rapids: William B. Eerdmans Company, 1955), pp. 108-24; *TDNT* 1,175, 18.

144. Nee, *Spiritual Man*, 1:61.

145. Idem, *Christian Life*, p. 16. See idem *Spiritual Man*, 1:76.

146. Idem, *Spiritual Man*, 1:77-82; idem, *Christian Life*, p. 24.

147. Idem, *Spiritual Man*, p. 133.

148. Rom. 6:6. Quoted in Nee, *Christian Life*, p. 40; idem, *Spiritual Man*, 1:78.

149. Rom. 6:11. See Nee, *Christian Life*, pp. 45-60; idem, *Spiritual Man* 1:137, 199.

150. Ibid., p. 135.

151. Idem, *Living Sacrifice*, pp. 51-66; idem, *Christian Life*, pp. 70-75.

152. Idem, *Living Sacrifice*, pp. 52-53.

153. Idem, *Christian Life*, p. 73.

154. Ibid., p. 71.

155. Ibid., 74-75; idem, *Living Sacrifice*, p. 62.

156. Ibid.

157. Idem, *Christian Life*, pp. 143f.

158. Ibid., pp. 76-85; idem, *Spiritual Man*, 1:44-46.

159. Idem, *Christian Life*, p. 80.

160. See pp. 38-40 supra.

161. On traditional Pentecostal theology see Hollenweger, *The Pentecostals*, pp. 321-52; Frederic Dale Bruner, *A Theology of the Holy Spirit* (Grand Rapids: William B. Eerdmans Publishing Company, 1970), passim; and Ralph M. Riggs, *The Spirit Himself* (Springfield, Mo.: Gospel Publishing Company, 1949), passim. For a Neo-Pentecostal approach see Howard M. Ervin, *These Are Not Drunken as Ye Suppose* (Plainfield, N.J.: Logos International, 1968), passim; Charles E. Hummel, *Fire in the Fireplace: Contemporary Charismatic Renewal* (Downers Grove, Ill.: Inter-Varsity Press, 1978), pp. 53-190; and Thomas A. Small, *Reflected Glory: The Spirit in Christ and Christians* (Grand Rapids: William B. Eerdmans Publishing Company, 1975), pp. 76-103. For a brief survey of both theologies see Russel Spittler, ed., *Perspectives on the New Pentecostalism* (Grand Rapids: Baker Book House, 1976), pp. 57-104.

162. Nee, *Christian Life*, pp. 87-92.

163. Ibid., pp. 95-97.

164. Ibid., pp. 94, 97.

165. Ibid., p. 101.

166. Ibid.

167. Ibid., pp. 106-121.

168. Quoted in ibid., p. 108.

169. Ibid., p. 114.

170. Gal. 2:20, quoted in ibid., p. 9.

171. Idem, *Spiritual Man,* 1:103.

172. Ibid., 2:246.

173. Ibid., 3:41.

174. Ibid., p. 132.

175. Ibid., p. 217.

176. Nee, *Release,* pp. 14-15.

177. Idem, *Living Sacrifice,* pp. 67-82; idem, *Search,* passim.

178. Idem, *Ministry,* passim.

179. Idem, *Living Sacrifice,* pp. 83-97; idem., *Prayer Ministry,* passim.

180. Idem, *Living Sacrifice,* pp. 99-115.

181. Idem, *Do All to the Glory of God,* Basic Lesson series, vol. 3 [trans., Stephen Kaung.] (New York: Christian Fellowship Publishers, Inc., 1974), pp. 1-45.

182. Idem, *Good Confession,* pp. 97-114.

183. Ibid., pp. 55-96.

184. Ibid., pp. 15-33; idem, *Love Not,* passim.

185. Idem, *Do All,* pp. 197-214.

186. Ibid., pp. 153-174.

187. See chapter 5.

CHAPTER FIVE

The Church and Its Work

Historical Considerations

As we stated in chapter three of this book, conversion begins with the basic revelation of the gospel.* In most instances this revelation is transmitted through the proclamation of the word by members of a local church. Nee taught that the mere recitation of doctrine is not enough, however; for the word is also spiritual and must be communicated by spiritual men.† Thus whenever the church no longer had spiritual descendants committed to a personal faith in Christ, it was because the church had not produced men of the spirit.

Nee applauded the efforts of missionaries in China for producing many converts, but Nee faulted them for not producing men of the spirit, enabled by the grace of God to continue church growth independent of foreign missionaries.[1] Nee's solution was to produce a new church intent upon producing spiritual men and therefore a church of the Spirit.

Nee's concept of the church is perhaps the most controversial portion of his overall theology. Many who have wholeheartedly accepted his ideas on Bible study and his concept of spirit/soul/body relationships have been reluctant to accept various aspects of his teachings on the church.

One book has already been written on the subject of Nee's church, James Mo-Oi Cheung's *The Ecclesiology of Watchman Nee and Witness Lee*. The book, originally written as a Master's thesis at Trinity Evangelical Divinity School, was suspended from sales shortly after its publication in 1972. As A. Donald Fredlund's letter states,* Mr. Cheung had made a serious error by consciously or unconsciously assigning Watchman Nee's *The Glorious Church* to Witness Lee. Despite this mistake, Mr. Cheung has demonstrated that much of the Nee/Lee ecclesiology is derived from Plymouth Brethren theology and shares its tendency towards ecclesiastical exclusiveness.

Both Nee and Lee take care in distinguishing themselves from the Brethren in the matter of the ground of the local church. According to Nee's own testimony between 1921 and 1932, "What the Lord revealed to me was extremely clear: before long He would raise local churches in various parts of China. Whenever I closed my eyes, the vision of the birth of local churches appeared before my inward eyes."[2] What Nee is saying here and what is most explicit throughout his ecclesiastical works is that the local church of God cannot be further defined through adjectives such as Pentecostal, Nazarene, Episcopal, Roman Catholic, Protestant, or even "gathered" as the Brethren did. It is only defined by the term, *local*: its locality. Yet, the basis of this teaching is very much an adjunct, if not a theological expansion of the Brethren teaching on "the one assembly of God." C.H. Mackintosh, one of the greatest writers in Brethren theology, in his book *The Assembly of God* writes:

> We must now very briefly glance at what is the power by which the assembly is gathered. Here, again, man and his doings are set aside. It is not man's will, choosing; nor man's reason, discovering; nor man's judgment, dictating;

---

* See Appendix A.

nor man's conscience, demanding; it is the Holy Ghost gathering souls to Jesus. As Jesus is the only center, so the Holy Ghost is the only gathering power. The one is as independent of man as the other. It is "where two or three are *gathered*" [sic]. It does not say "where two or three are *met*." Persons may meet together round any centre, on any ground, by any influence, and merely form a club, a society, an association, a community. But the Holy Ghost gathers souls to Jesus on the ground of salvation; and this, wherever convened, is the principle of the Assembly of God, and nothing else is. It may consist of but "two or three," and there may be hundreds of Christians in the various religious systems around; yet would the "two or three" be on the ground of the Assembly of God.[3]

Nee was quite familiar with C.H. Mackintosh's writings, and he in fact presents arguments for an assembly ecclesiology in his *Assembly Together*.[4] Regardless of this Brethren "truth," Nee believed that to establish this doctrine as the basis of church fellowship was just as carnal as those established on the abilities of spiritual leaders or racial, material or social distinction within a local area.[5] Rather when God gathered His people in the New Testament, it was always on the basis of the location named: Corinth, Ephesus, Rome, etc. And since every believer has the same Spirit of Christ within himself, every Christian must demonstrate the unity of that Spirit by attending one body in one locality. Latent within this view, though not explicitly expressed by Nee, is a dividing between those who listen to the unifying Spirit and join the local church movement and those who do not join the movement and are therefore not in tune with the Spirit's leading—between spiritual men and carnal men.*

Such a strong stand cannot be explained entirely by theological and exegetical considerations. Like many Chinese leaders[7] Nee was intolerant towards the interdenominational

---

* One of his successors, Witness Lee, is more explicit.[6]

rivalries. The disparity between the church's faith in the unity of the body of Christ and its own defense of sectarianism was exaggerated by foreign colonialists who detested the high standards of missionaries and Chinese anti-imperialist sentiments. In truth, the Christian community in China had a greater degree of "ecumenical spiritual unity" than was evident in America or England at the time. Because they were a minority and they had all suffered persecution during the Boxer Rebellion, denominations were less important; faith more. Ministry among the differing denominations by fellowshipping "spiritually was common."* The opportunity to bring Christ to China enabled most Christians to "stretch out their hands over the fence to hold hands on the other side." Nee rebuffed those who offered such a solution:

> We cannot on the one hand covet fellowship and yet on the other hand have fellowship over fences. If we really desire fellowship, we must break down the fences and have fellowship. If we want to serve God and feel that all God's children should have fellowship, we must tear down all the fences to have fellowship. If the fences are right, then we must build the fences, not only ten feet high, but ten thousand feet high. We must be thorough and absolute before God.

For Nee, the solution was to tear down the denominational fences and accept the spiritual and physical fellowship of his local churches—forming a single church denomination divided only on the basis of locality, as the churches are denominated in the New Testament.

---

* Most notably the China Inland Mission. During the 1939 Keswick Conference in England, Watchman Nee prayed for unity among Chinese and Japanese Christians. The Director of the China Inland Mission was impressed. Upon his visit to China, he chastised CIM missionaries for criticizing Nee. What he did not know is that Nee saw fit keep secret his anti-denominational rhetoric at the Keswick Interdenominational Conference. [8]

As a gifted national leader in the Chinese church, Nee had the choice of either staying within the existing denominations or becoming an independent church. Either way, the opportunity was there for Nee to choose his own ecclesiology, as well as the ecclesiology of his fellow workers and the flocks under his tutorial care.

His radical "Brethren" approach was most certainly motivated by one historical consideration: his thorough education in the spiritual piety of the Keswick and Brethren movements. From Brethren writers came the administrative outline of *The Normal Christian Church Life*; from Keswick speakers he identified the life of the church within the life of Christ emanating not from the carnal believer but from the spiritual man.

The Church Universal

Watchman Nee's concept of the church universal is very much a product of his central focus on the cross and its work upon the trichotomous man. "If we know the cross," Nee wrote, "in the way in which God means it to be known, we shall eventually find oneself within the Body [the Church]."[10] Since the first knowledge we receive about the cross—that Christ died for our sins—comes at conversion, Nee agreed with the Brethren theology that the minimum requirement for church fellowship and membership in the church is salvation, the presence of Christ's Spirit in man. The mere mental assent of man's soul was not enough. Membership comes as a result of revelation intuitively received by our quickened spirits.[11]

Conversion and membership in the church are also synonymous, because the church is Christ. Beyond that, the nature and life of the church is to bring the exalted Christ unto the entire man. The church therefore is simultaneously fully Christ in its state and not fully Christ in its status. Nee explains the seemingly contradictory statement by seeing in the Bible two "Christs." The personal Christ is exalted upon the throne and has already won the victory. The corporate Christ, which is the personal Christ and the church, has not yet experienced the final victory. Only by the edification of the church through the proclamation of God's Word and its resurrection in the *eschaton* can the church experience the full status of the personal exalted Christ.[12]

This close synonymity of Christ with the church is also present in Nee's discussion of the "Eve" typology of Eph. 5:22-32.[13] Since the church is Eve, he contends:

> The Church is composed only of that which is out of Christ. All man's talent, ability, thought, self, and all that he has are outside the Church. Everything which comes from the natural man is outside the Church. Only that which comes out of Christ is in the Church. Eve was not made from clay, but from Adam, the one who typified Christ. The preciousness is that God took a rib from Adam and made Eve. Only that which came from Adam, not from clay, can be called "Eve," and only that which comes out from Christ can be called the Church. All that is not from Christ has nothing to do with the Church.[14]

As a corollary to his assertion that the fleshly labors of carnal Christians are not a part of the church, the church universal is understood as originating from the sinless flesh of Christ and is therefore entirely sinless.

The Church Local

Perhaps the greatest weakness or failing in Watchman Nee's theology is in the practical expression of Christ's kingdom in the local church. While the underlying policies toward the church universal remained constant, his techniques of the church local underwent a serious change, in some instances a volte-face from his earlier prewar teachings. This ecclesiological change has also created a division within the present-day local church movement and generally a division between churches who favor the doctrines present in *The Normal Christian Church Life, What Shall This Man Do?* and *The Glorious Church*, and those who adhere to the teachings present in *The Orthodoxy of the Church, Spiritual Authority* and *Further Talks on the Church Life.*

Nee's vision of the local church life style in the three earlier writings is most assuredly motivated by two concerns: a reexamination of the witness of Scripture and a theological interpretation of church history. What comes forth is the image of the church whose life is generated by the Holy Spirit in the life of man and is independent of any carnal ideologies.

The local church is local because the New Testament offers no other basis for division, according to Nee. Because it includes every Christian in a given restricted, geographical area* and because it has no authority over other churches, Nee feels that the church is safeguarded against a sectarian spirit. "... there is no scope for an able and ambitious false prophet to display his organizing genius by forming the different companies of believers into one fast federation and then satisfy his ambition by constituting himself as its head."[16] Theological heresies† are also in a sense quarantined to one church by reason of the church's isolationist polity.

In the defining of church offices, Nee is also careful that each ministry be compartmentalized in a way that presumedly will not interfere in the spiritual life of the church. The first office defined in *The Normal Christian Church Life* is that of the apostle or, as perceived in the contemporary age, the missionary. As a Christian involved in the extralocal activity

---

* Nee defines local as a town or, in the case of a large city, a borough.[15]
† These include divisions on the basis of spiritual superheroes, the instrument of salvation, anti-sectarianism, doctrinal differences, and racial, national, and social differences.[17]

of the gospel, the missionary's authoritative sphere is uniquely governed by what Nee describes as the "Antioch" model of church growth. In Acts 13, Paul and Barnabas were commissioned by the Holy Spirit to establish other local churches. As apostles, they could not rule at Antioch, for they were appointed to an extralocal ministry. Likewise, they could not be elders in the churches they founded; but they could appoint elders in the new congregations. In this, Nee believed that the Holy Spirit had established a ministry model that preserved the local character of the church—even the newly formed churches.

Within the church local, the elders/bishops, appointed by the Holy Spirit in due season, rule over the congregation. The two primary qualifications for an elder are that he be a member of the church there and that he be spiritually mature. This necessitates the Spirit's work in the congregation and in the apostles; personal preference must not interfere in the selection. Once appointed, the elders rule and manage the work of the congregation. They can even refuse an apostle's entry into the assembly hall.[18]

In the governing policies of the local church, Nee makes every effort to ensure that all things be done by the Spirit of God and not with any carnal motives. For example, businesses, hospitals, schools, charitable institutions, and even Christian ministries must not be a part of the church. While these jobs can and should be done by spiritual men, they cannot detract from the real responsibilities of the church, being "the conducting of meetings for breaking of bread, for the exercise of spiritual gifts, for the study of the Word, for prayer, for fellowship and Gospel preaching."[19] No worker— whether he be an elder, an apostle, or a holder of any office— may receive a salary. He must live according to the free-will gifts received from Spirit-led brethren.

Underlying Nee's principle of church government is a strong reluctance to accept any form of organization. Instead, the church must be an organism dependent on the Spirit for its life. Even such faith missions as the China Inland Mission Nee suspected of having workers not entirely dependent on faith. For if one member lives by his faith in such "faith" missions, he must equally share what God has provided to the less faithful in the corporate mission structure. In summary, what emerges in these earlier writings is a decentralized, highly evangelistic movement originating out of Nee's concern for a rigid biblicism and that, "Everything which comes from the natural man is outside the church."[20]

However, the managerial policies avowed as biblical in *The Orthodoxy of the Church, Spiritual Authority,* and *Further Talks on the Church Life* entirely differ from Nee's earlier writings and are reflective of differing historical circumstances. The church is no longer seeking to establish itself as a new theological front in a pagan society. Rather it is now an established church attempting to recover from the church's instability during the Japanese occupation, from the tempering of Nee's teaching authority as a result of his business entanglements at his brother's chemical firm, and from the growing influence of Witness Lee. While these three books bear the imprimatur of Nee's name as author and his homiletical style, the organizational activism of Witness Lee is strongly present. It is Lee, described by Kinnear as "energetic and authoritarian, thriving on large numbers, and has a flair for organizing people,"[21] who is responsible for much of Nee's new ecclesiology that runs counter to Nee's earlier teachings. In the early local church, it is the spiritual man, revealed out of Nee's own sufferings and Bible studies, who rules the congregation. But according to Witness Lee's authoritarian personality, in the postwar era, it is the spiritual man that takes charge in the local church.

In *The Orthodoxy of the Church*, the second and third chapters of Revelation are interpreted in a way that is critical of all other churches except the "local church." Written at a time when he was excommunicated from the Shanghai Church and Lee was his most faithful co-worker, Nee castigates Roman Catholics as the church of Thyatira, Protestants as Sardis, and many of the Brethren as Laodicea. Nee's arguments are based on interpreting church history as a progressive recovery of the original truths of the Ephesus and Smyrna churches. While Nee always regarded other denominations with disfavor,* he here brings eschatological judgment upon all other churches:

> The Lord Jesus is the priest who walks in the midst of the churches to see which lamp is lighted and which one is not. The trimming is the judgment, for the judgment begins in the house of God. Christ walks in the midst of the churches doing the work of judgment, and today's judgment is seen from eternity.[23]

> All those who study the Bible know that the problem of choosing the Roman Catholic Church is over. The difficulty lies here: that is, many brothers do not know that the problem of choosing the Protestant churches is also over. Does the Lord want us to be in Sardis? Strangely enough, many are rather satisfied to be in Sardis. But as we read the Word of God, the Lord will show us that He is not satisfied with Sardis. The Lord's desire is Philadelphia.[24]

According to Nee's book, only some Brethren and the local church are the faithful overcomers who are the church of Philadelphia. Here the words of Nee are "spiritual" in sound as are his earlier writings, but a bitter note rings now.

In chapter six of *Further Talks on the Church Life*, the doctrine of Jerusalem principle is presented. According to

---

* Nee's anti-denominationalism created problems among co-workers as early as 1923.[22]

this "light" of God's truth, the work of the church is regional, and therefore the work must proceed not from every local church, but from a regional center.[25] According to this plan, workers from the differing congregations go to one of these regional centers and are trained for two months to one year. From there they either return to their own local churches as leaders or go off to one of the unchurched mission fields. Out of experiences learned during the war years, missionaries are now sent out or "migrated" in groups of twenty to forty.[26]

In this same chapter, while offering his continuing support of the revelation of "locality," Nee nullifies the practical reality of the local churches' independence. Nee tells his trainees, "Therefore, brothers, when you, a co-worker, reside in a locality, you are there as both an apostle and an elder."[27] Thus the regional center governs all other local churches, not through an episcopal control, as is the case in Roman Catholic, Episcopal, and Methodist churches, but through a pedagogic control.

The dynamics of this polity work on the principle that there are spiritual men capable of teaching others to do the "work." As practiced in the postwar local church in China, there are actually only two "spiritual men" who are doing the teaching: Watchman Nee and Witness Lee. Whether a co-worker trained in the regional center at Shanghai or Foochow, the training lessons were the same—standardized by Nee's and Lee's revelations on the meaning of God's Word. Then a group of these newly trained co-workers would be sent into the local church to increase the church's membership and aid the old members with their spiritual teachings. Invariably they did increase the membership more rapidly than the less organized methods of the independent local church. By their successful efforts and with the support of the new members, these trained co-workers became the new elders of the expanding local church, and they are able

to over-ride the decisions of the older elders. While the Nee/
Lee takeover usually went smoothly, the local church in
Foochow split in two in 1948, and through Witness Lee's
efforts, the Hong Kong local church became bitterly divided
over the admission of co-workers as elders in 1970.[28]

Added to this was a new dimension to the importance of
the spiritual man in the local church movement. Prior to this
period, it was understood that all the differing works of grace
were open to all, and everyone was capable of reaching the
highest earthly plateau of Christian maturity. But in the new
local church, a spiritual hierarchy was unconsciously being
established with Watchman Nee first, then Witness Lee, then
the workers/elders taught at one of the training centers, then
the rest of the men, and finally the women, who must wear
veils out of submission.[29] Kinnear even reports that a row of
chairs were set up in each meeting place for the top echelon,
in which the number one seat was unanimously reserved
for Nee.[30] The theological-spiritual basis for this development
was given to co-workers during their training and is preserved
in the book *Spiritual Authority*.

In *Spiritual Authority*, Nee argues that to disobey the
authorities delegated by God in the church (e.g., elders) and
in the world is to disobey and be in rebellion against God:

> People will perhaps argue, "What if the authority is
> wrong?" The answer is, If God dares to entrust His authority
> to men, then we can dare to obey. Whether the one in
> authority is right or wrong does not concern us, since he
> has to be responsible directly to God. The obedient needs
> only to obey; the Lord will not hold us responsible for any
> mistaken obedience, rather will He hold the delegated
> authority responsible for his erroneous act. Insubordination,
> however, is rebellion, and for this the one under authority
> must answer to God.[31]

Mozi or the Holy Spirit?

In Chinese philosophy, political authority is authority delegated from the emperor, Son of Heaven. The Son of Heaven can't do the work of governing the world all on his own. He set up a system of superiors and subordinates. Superiors are chosen by The Son because they are best able to rule wisely. To disagree with them and to undermine their position is to challenge Heaven itself. Mozi (470-391 B.C.) says:

Whenever you hear of something good or bad, always inform your superior. Whenever your superior approves of something as right you too must approve of it. Whenever your superior condemns something as wrong you too must condemn it.[32]

At first glance, the idea seems sound and biblical. Doesn't Hebrew 3:17 say, "Obey your leaders and submit to their authority. They keep watch over you as men who must give an account. Obey them so that their work will be a joy, not a burden, for that would be of no advantage to you."? Yet, there are limits to any man's authority. Every Christian is on a journey of faith. The church and its leaders are there to feed, not to force feed, the grace of God. Ultimately the believer surrenders his thoughts and actions to God and not to a holy man. The shepherds of God's flock feed Christ's sheep, not rule them (John 21:16).

Yet, disrespect for trained Christian leaders is a serious problem in many churches. Many American churches remain small because they shoot the messenger . . . figuratively. After a few years of ministry, the church begins to grow under a new pastor's leadership. The older leadership resents his success. They feel threatened by the presence of new members who may not agree with current church policies. Often the church leaders, who first welcomed the new pastor "as a man of God," are eager to see him leave. Spiritual authority is not as important as keeping it "their church."

Nee also enumerates the characteristics that he expects to be found in God's delegated authorities. A total of five pages is devoted to the ethical requirements of eldership; a total of seventy pages is devoted to the spiritual qualifications.

The Church in the Eschaton

Much of what Nee presents in his biblical anthropological texts tends toward a kind of bifurcation between the spiritual and carnal Christian. In the eschatology of *Come, Lord Jesus, God's Plan and the Overcomers,* and *Love Not the World,* the final destination of the church is also divided between the saved and the "overcomers":

> Only the overcoming believers are related to the new city during the millennial kingdom. In the new heaven and new earth, both the saved and the overcomers partake equally in New Jerusalem.
>
> The wedding gown is worn only for a time; the believers who overcome are joined together as the bride.
>
> At the marriage of the Lamb, it looks as though the door of the New Jerusalem is opened for the first time to let in the overcomers. The foolish virgins are not able to enter at this time.[32]

In support of this, Nee identifies the 144,000 in Rev. 7:4-8 as the Jews who will rule with Christ; the 144,000 in 14:1 are the overcoming "virgins" who are representative of the larger group of "overcomers" in the church. While the former will reign with Christ among the nations during the millennium, the latter are caught up in the air and simultaneously reign in the heavenlies.[33] While all Christians have a place in the new heaven and earth, only these overcomers enter into the new Jerusalem during the 1,000 years.

Since the "overcomers" are a prominent part of the seven letters of Revelation 2 and 3, Nee presupposes that in the modern church, only those who have experienced the historic

The Church and Its Work

recovery of the Philadelphia church—the spiritual Christians of the Brethren and local church movements—will share in the heavenly millennial reign of Christ.

In both *Love Not the World* and *God's Plan and the Overcomers* Nee draws on the overcoming imagery of Revelation to affirm victory over Satan, the prince of this world. But the victory over Satan in the world "demands an utterness of spirit Godward that in itself effectively deprives Satan of any moral ground in us he may claim to possess."[34] Because they are spiritually mature, not only will the overcomers share Christ's kingdom in the coming age, but they will also institute that reign by ascending to heaven in the rapture:

> When they are on earth, Satan has no retreat; and when they ascend to heaven, Satan is cast down. Victory lies in regaining the ground. The man child conquers on behalf of the mother [Rev. 12:5-10]: the overcomers win the victory for the church. Moreover, in the end time, God uses overcomers to conclude the war in heaven. These overcomers shall bring "the salvation, and the power, and the kingdom of our God, and the authority of his Christ" into heaven. The serpent therefore has no more place in heaven. Hence wherever the overcomers are, Satan is forced to retreat.[35]

The judicial division between the carnal saved and the spiritual overcomers is also applied to the believer's present resting place after death. Pressed by the need to make distinctions between believers, Nee is forced into accepting a Protestant form of purgatory. When questioned about the people in Heb. 6:4-6 in the book *Gospel Dialogue*, Nee interprets the context as dealing with Christian progress and not with a falling away from salvation. Accordingly, the people in Hebrews 6 are identified as Christians living in sin according to works who must be refined through a limited period of punishment.[36]

I Don't Know

Who exactly are the overcomers? The church has generally understood them to be the people who remained faithful to God in spite of the opportunities and temptations of adultery, going back to legally protected Judaism, and the teaching of the Nicolaitans. Who are the Nicolaitans (Rev. 2:6, 15)? I don't know.

The best historical evidence suggests that they were a group within and outside the church. In *Contra Haereses* 3.11.7, Irenaeus, a second century Christian writer, says they were one of the Gnostic groups who believed that salvation came in knowing divine secrets. To say that it refers to Christian groups who believe in strong elder leadership, such as the local church, is speculation. Whatever the group's teaching, it does deny the grace of Christ to overcome the world (John 1:5).

Admittedly, the identification of the overcomers with Nee's spiritual men is not directly stated in any of his eschatological discourses. Nevertheless, the identification is communicated by his use of the same idioms and expressions of his spiritual anthropology in his description of the overcomers. For example, since the work of the cross also divides overcomers from the rest of the saved,[37] it is most certain that the carnal/spiritual division of believers is synonymous or parallel to his eschatological dichotomy of overcomers and other Christians. Historically this is again in evidence in the close tie with Nee's spiritual life/man teachings and his partial rapture theory. M.E. Barber, who tutored Nee in the Keswick approach to spiritual dynamics, assuredly taught him a partial rapture theory. For the theory originated in the writings of Robert Govett (1813-1901), who, after leaving the Anglican Church, founded Surry Chapel,

Norwich. As was stated in chapter one, Miss Barber was sent out from this same chapel as an independent missionary. Nee even admits in his lecture on the Book of Revelation, published as *Come, Lord Jesus*, his dependence on Govett's *The Apocalypse Expounded* (1920)[38]—no doubt borrowed from Miss Barber's library.

The Name Game

Out of its Plymouth Brethren heritage in England and anti-missionary sentiments in China, the churches established by Watchman Nee declare themselves free from denominationalism. They see themselves free from the division described in 1 Corinthians 1. They did this by declaring that the basis for establishing a church can only be locality. But if denominationalism is the real sin occurring in Corinth then locality didn't help. Paul wrote to one locality: The church in Corinth. In that local church were divisions or denominations into groups supporting different teachers.

Indeed Nee had to deal with divisions within his own local churches. In July of 1934, a Miss Ding Shu-shin disagreed with the Local church policy requiring women to wear head coverings. Nee's response was strict: Miss Ding is a woman. Women are not allowed to teach. Even though the Foochow church is a local church it must submit to the decision of the Shanghai Church. The Shanghai Church is more spiritual. If they don't agree, then the senior church says they can be excommunicated.[39]

Chapter 5 Endnotes

1. Kinnear, *Against the Tide*, pp. 34, 56.

2. Nee, *Testimony*, p. 31.

3. C.H. Mackintosh, *The Assembly of God*, pp. 35ff. Quoted in William Reid, *Plymouth Brethrenism: Unveiled and Refuted* (Edinburgh: William Oliphant & Company, 1880), p. 57.

4. Nee, *Assembly*, pp. 33-42.

5. Idem, *Church Life*, pp. 65-71.

6. Lee, *Christ vs. Religion*, passim.

7. Allen J. Swanson, *Taiwan: Mainline versus Independent Church Growth: A Study in Contrasts* (S. Pasedena, Cal.: William Carey Library, 1970), pp. 16-64.

8. Lyall, *Mighty Men*, passim. Lee, *Watchman*, p. 176. Lee, *Nee*, p. 176.

9. Nee, *Further Talks*, pp. 96ff.

10. Nee, *What Shall This Man Literature Do?* (Fort Washington, Pa.: Christian Crusade, 1961), p. 71.

11. Ibid., p. 77.

12. Idem, *Christ the Sum*, p. 59; idem, *Love One Another*, p. 194.

13. Idem, *The Glorious Church*, pp. 27-45.

14. Ibid., pp. 31ff.

15. Nee, *Church Life*, pp. 47-49.

16. Ibid., pp. 56-57.

17. Ibid., pp. 64-71.

18. Ibid., p. 41.

19. Ibid., p. 75.

20. Idem, *The Glorious Church*, pp. 31ff.

21. Kinnear, *Against the Tide*, p. 131.

22. Kinnear, *Against the Tide*, pp. 55-58; Lo-Shan [pseud.], "From

'The Case of Fraud in the Church': To See the Conspiracy of the Church at the Secret Organization, Part One," *Nan Pei Chi* 32 (January 16, 1973):37.

23. Nee, *Orthodoxy*, p. 14.

24. Ibid., p. 101.

25. Idem, *Further Talks*, p. 155.

26. Ibid., pp. 159-62.

27. Ibid., p. 159.

28. Kinnear, *Against the Tide*, p. 138; Cheung, *Ecclesiology*, p. 26; Lo-Shan [pseud.]. "From 'The Case of Fraud in the Church': To See the Conspiracy of the Church by the Secret Organization, Part Three," *Nan Pei Chi* 34 (March 10, 1973):58-59.

29. Watchman Nee, *Spiritual Authority* (New York: Christian Fellowship Publishers, 1972), p. 67.

30. Kinnear, *Against the Tide*, p. 139.

31. Nee, *Authority*, p. 71.

32. Philip J. Ivanhoe and Bryan W. Van Norden, *Readings in Classical Chinese Philosphy* (New York: Seven Bridges Press, 2001), p. 61.

32. Idem, *"Come,"* p. 208.

33. Ibid., pp. 153-57.

34. Idem, *Love Not*, p. 86.

35. Idem, *God's Plan and the Overcomers* (New York: Christian Fellowship Publishers, 1977), p. 82. Cf. Idem, *Gospel Dialogue*, pp. 58, 88-89.

36. Idem, *Gospel Dialogue*, p. 157.

37. Idem, *God's Plan*, p. 61.

38. Idem, *"Come,"* p. 62.

39. Watchman Nee, *Conferences, Messages, and Fellowship. 6 vols.* (Anaheim, Ca: Living Stream Ministry, 1997-2005. http://www.minstrybooks.org/collected-works.html.), Volume 1, Chapter 6.

Summary and Conclusions

The first chapter of this book presented a number of historical details quite significant in understanding and appreciating Nee's theology. Reared in a cultural setting that was both Oriental and an admixture of Occidental practice and Christian proclamation, Nee's conversion and early ministry were marked by his own struggle of conscience between biblical demand and human practice. First, Nee despaired over his inability to serve the Lord in conformance to the witness of Scripture and the convictions of his conscience. Secondly, his mind was preoccupied with finding some way of purifying the evangelical witness in China of any purely Western, non-biblical elements. The first conflict Nee resolved during a lengthy illness by discriminating between "carnal" and "spiritual" believers on the basis of their appropriation of the work of the cross of Christ. The second goal resulted in his establishment of a new indigenous church based on the principle of "locality" and "spiritual" leadership. While he changed some of his views on the church, both Nee and his successors continued to distinguish between the "carnal" and the "spiritual" side of Christian faith.

In chapter two, the style and content of his literature were examined for evidence of continuity. Whether it be in the early years of his career or in the last years before his imprisonment, all of his material was written or spoken in a devotional, expository form that emphasized the "spiritual reality" of the Bible and the "normal Christian life."

The succeeding three chapters offered an analysis of Nee's fundamental teachings. Like Karl Barth, Nee is deeply concerned with the Word of God both as Scripture and as church proclamation. On the basis of his belief in God's perfecting grace in the life of the spiritually minded, he concludes that the interpretation and preaching of Scripture can be inerrant in its communication of spiritual life. Far more elaborate and complex than his writings on the Word, his teachings on anthropology are also based on a trichotomous division of man into spirit, soul, and body. Without these elements being in proper relationship with one another and with God, Nee contends, the normal Christian life is impossible. Likewise, the church's life cannot be normal unless it is structured in a way that produces spiritual men and excludes the heresy and divisions brought about by the "soulish" or carnal believer. In fact, the ultimate destination of the church is divided between those who are merely saved and those who are "spiritual."

On the basis of historical and literary research, therefore, certain conclusions can be drawn concerning the nature and significance of Watchman Nee as a church leader and expositor:

1. The growing need for reform in the church of China serves as the historical *Sitz im Leben* ("life situation") for Nee's beliefs. The indigenous movement within the church and anti-missionary sentiments without are important factors in understanding the radical content and direction of Nee's teachings.

2. The reform of the church through the spiritual reform of the Christian offered by Nee and the Local Church originated in Nee's tutelage in Keswick and Brethren theology.

3. Concern for the spiritual condition of the believer is a persistent theme throughout Nee's preaching career.

4. In Nee's theology, Scripture can only be comprehended, communicated and perceived as the living Word of God by means of an intrapsychic working of the Holy Spirit in the believer.

5. The Christian is a trichotomous being. By the Holy Spirit quickening a man's fallen spirit, the believer is a union of body, soul and spirit. Each element has its own functions and its own requirements for spiritual health.

6. The Christian life, which Nee deems "normal," comes by the differential working of grace on the spirit, soul and body.

7. The church consists of both spiritual and carnal Christians.

8. The New Testament church is interpreted as having a structure that inhibited the works of the carnal believer (heresies, sectarianism, etc.) and encouraged the works of the spiritual believer. In Nee's thought that structure was governed either by the principle of "locality" or by the pedagogic authority of the spiritual man.

9. At Christ's return, the spiritual Christians who have overcome the world will play a different part in the millennial reign than will the carnally minded believers. The spiritual man will reign with Christ in the heavenlies; the carnal man will reign with Christ on earth among the nations.

In summary, driven by an intense desire to have more of Christ's life and power manifest in China, Nee's notion of the spiritual man became the determinate foundation that gave substance to his doctrine of revelation, Scripture, sanctification, perfection, ecclesiology and eschatology.

An Evangelical Assessment

To read any of the books ascribed to Watchman Nee is sure to create strong opinions as to the potential value of his ideas. During the past five years, I have interviewed many pastors, teachers, seminary students and informed laymen in order to find some majority consensus. Some praised Nee for his insights into the nature of the Christian church and its spiritual life. A few described how churches have experienced renewal as a result of studying one or more of his books. Yet, others upbraided Nee for false doctrine and unconsciously providing a convenient theology for such cult groups as The Way, The Children of God and The Alamo Foundation. A few described how spiritual pride, fostered by Nee's division of spiritual and carnal believers, had divided congregations.

The ambiguity of these responses gives some indication that a simple dismissal or unqualified support of Watchman Nee is inappropriate. Watchman Nee was unquestionably a witness imprisoned because of the Word of God and the testimony he maintained. Yet, as a writer within the broad spectrum of evangelicalism read largely by evangelicals, Nee's teaching and preaching legacy should be subject to the plumb line of God's Word, the Bible. Upon this basis, certain of Nee's doctrines and presuppositions are certainly questionable.

Nee is admirable and insightful in understanding the illuminating work of divine revelation in comprehending the spiritual reality of the Bible. But he also seems unappreciative of the Bible as God's interpretation of real events, language, culture and people in His covenant history. In Nee's discussions of Bible study methods, comparing and compiling texts are his keys to understanding, never the historical circumstances of the passages. Like many writers who rely entirely on the devotional hermeneutic, he never subjects the biblical text to some discerning questions: Why does the author say this? How does it fit into the context of the whole book? Does the historical background of the passage relate to the circumstances of my own life or the life of my church?

Particularly in interpreting anthropological terms, Nee's method is far too often a lexical search through Young's or Cruden's concordance, where historical or literary context is not under consideration. In 1 Thess. 5:23, for example, is Paul making a statement about biblical anthropology or is he using the language of his opponents? The latter does more justice to the biblical evidence. Paul is writing to a church unable to fit physical death and physical labor into their theology. We know for certain that some forms of Greek gnostic philosophy during this period saw the spirit in opposition to the limitations of the soul and body.*

If Paul is opposing the syncretizing of this view with Christian faith, then 1 Thess. 5:23 is not saying that spirit, soul and body are entirely distinct human entities. Rather, Paul is saying that the ongoing sanctification in Christ until the second coming involves the whole man ("through and through").

Or Heb. 4:12. Is the dividing asunder by the Word of God a distinguishing of two parts of man's nature (soul and spirit), as Nee contends? Or does the dividing of the Word of God involve a judgment on whether the thoughts and attributes of the heart are from man (soul) or from God (Spirit)? The entire context of Hebrews 4 suggests that we are dealing with the motives of the heart, not with some intrapsychic battle of a human spirit with the soul.

This compilation of proof texts apart from the rigors of understanding context is certainly compatible to the "amen's"

---

* That gnosticism is at issue here is evident in that "soul" in a psychological sense appears only in Paul's letters to the Thessalonians and Corinthians where belief in a future, physical, resurrection was a problem.

of the spiritually enlightened. But there are dangers to such an understanding of Scripture. First, spiritual exegesis often leads to a "canon within the canon." Churches and movements that have entirely "sought" to touch the spiritual reality of the Bible through the prayer methods described in Nee's *The Ministry of God's Word* and *Ye Search the Scriptures* often neglect the narrative portions that deal with the humanness of God's revelation. There is no earthly life of Jesus discernible in the writings of Nee; rather it is the resurrected Christ of doctrinal theology that Nee continually homilizes. The historical books of the Old Testament are only touched upon whenever they use some anthropological terms or as they foreshadow the finished work of Christ. The prophets are discussed for their prediction of the redemptive future, not when they proclaim judgment upon the social injustices of their own age. While as a matter of evangelical faith Nee affirms the sixty-six books of the Bible, in practice his words have depicted the canon as a more spiritual, less historical book.

Secondly, Nee's historical and spiritual understanding of the Bible infers that the church's spiritual life is unconcerned with the physical reality of war, famine, and injustice. Like Jessie Penn-Lewis's magazine, *Overcomer*, Nee writes without reference to the inordinate suffering of the Chinese during World War II. While the social ethicists of modern liberalism ignore the spiritual dimension of God's kingdom, the pietism underlying Nee's view of Scripture has lost sight of the social concern of such passages as Amos 2:6-8, Luke 14:12-14 and James 5:1-5.

Finally Nee' spiritual exegesis, mixed with a shift toward a more monarchial form of government, led to the phenomena of Witness Lee and the Local Church. From the beginning, Watchman Nee's preaching eloquence led many to honor and admire him to a degree beyond the range of

. critical judgment or the New Testament's demand to test the spirits of events and teachings within the congregation. Those like Leland Wang, who disapproved, were never permitted any congregational expression of grievances, and inevitably left. Those who remained were more docile to the teachings of their elders and insensitive to the changes taking place in the church's doctrines and leadership.

Fundamentally, the idea of spiritual exegesis is not foreign to New Testament Christianity. Every believer to a varying degree has a tremendous advantage over the secular man in comprehending the Bible because of his relationship in Christ. Yet such a method of prayer and meditation opted by the spiritual exegete is not without its dangers. When the Christian message of the resurrection had become too spiritualized in the Corinthian community, Paul provided correction in the recounting of the history of Christ's resurrection appearances (1 Corinthians 15:3-9). Likewise, today, separated as we are by the cultural and historic changes of two millennia, both private and public proclamation must accord with the historic accounts and revelations given in the Bible within its cultural (Semitic and Hellenistic) setting.

Beyond the problem in biblical exegesis, Nee's discrimination between what is acceptably human, the spirit, and what is unacceptably human, the soul, in our spiritual life creates an introspective life. Christian faith is not perceived as a sacrificial offering of ourselves to God, a life "in Christ" and a community set apart from worldly values. Nee instead offers "laws of the spirit," definitions of soulical and spiritual, and mind analysis in order to receive full salvation.[1] While some of his works, like *The Normal Christian Life*, rightly have the cross as its bench mark, others, such as *The Latent Power of the Soul* and *The Spiritual Man*, teach us gnostic psychoanalysis. In the latter, the key to Christian maturity is not something easily discernible to the born-again believer.

Rather, by extensive Bible studies supplemented by the "spiritual knowledge" of the mature and a series of spiritual enlightenments, one can receive full salvation.

True spirituality, however, is an activity of the Holy Spirit and is therefore God's gracious gift. It can not be fulminated by obeying a list of psychic commandments. The Holy Spirit as sanctifier admonishes us whenever we are living according to our own desires (the flesh) and encourages us when we live according to God's will (the Spirit). Whether or not one understands the characteristics of the soul and the "human spirit" is irrelevant. Once sin is made known, continuing growth is conditioned upon repentance and surrendering ourselves more to the work of the Holy Spirit.[68]

Nee's description of the "carnal man" and the "soulical man" can and does quite powerfully expose that part of the Christian personality that continues to function by its own strength quite independently of God's power. It may therefore be even true that some intrapsychic law; are in operation. But it is altogether unnecessary to be able to recite them to serve God more abundantly. Indeed, sanctification preconditioned upon our comprehension of the hidden mechanics of the spiritual man may lead to a spirit of pride rather than to a humble and contrite heart.

It is this pride of knowledge which also flaws the quality of Nee's idea on the church and its life. In particular Nee's rejection of any local church that does not denominate itself on the basis of a geographical locality is another example of his hidden wisdom from the Bible. Followers of Witness Lee and Watchman Nee who have banded together to form "local churches" believe that the "recovery" of this doctrine makes them more faithful to Gods plan of the church. However, the Bible never commands us to label our churches in a

---

* Rom. 12:1.

particular way. The Bible does command and commend the fruits or works of righteousness by the power of Christ's Spirit within us.

Finally, we must fault Nee in his teachings on pastoral authority, a fault that has been the most destructive to the evangelical witness of Christ in the contemporary church. According to the Scriptures, the church's mission is to proclaim the King of kings and His kingdom, but Nee seems to have made God's lieutenants, the elders, local monarchs themselves. The local church elders described in *Spiritual Authority* have unquestioned authority. Such authoritativeness is inappropriate to God's elect, who proclaim God's sovereign rule in their lives. The Epistle to the Hebrews does say, "Obey them that have rule over you" (13:7). But to the author of Hebrews, obeying an elder is following his example by proclaiming the Word of God to others, emulating his Christian life, and imitating his faith in God (13:7). As the word "elder" implies, leaders arise in the church not by their dominating personality, nor by their preaching ability, but by the maturity of their relationship with Christ as Lord of their lives.

Nee's whole spiritual philosophy assumes that the mature who give direction are elected by God for their spiritual "charisma." A tranquil face, a peaceful smile and a spiritual aura that condescends to the "unspiritual" become the trademarks of the leader in such superspiritual churches. In contrast, Christ set an example for us, in the washing of the disciples' feet, of a leader who is a servant not a spiritual prince. While Nee's version of a charismatic leader appeals to the contemporary culture' quest and infatuation with the gnostic guru, it is not Christlike. What the church needs today are leaders who demonstrate to us the fruit of righteousness in the manner of one of God's faithful servants.

Nee himself became for some Christian readers a spiritual guru, a mystic intermediary between Christ and the struggling believer. For them he "recovered" the key to becoming spiritual. His style and message became a guide in determining the value of other Christian writers. Those that lacked the spiritual flavor of Nee's words were dismissed as carnal or tainted by the power of the soul.

But many more Christians read with a discerning eye. They did not enjoy or agree with every book ascribed to Watchman Nee. They read books by Christians of different literary styles and temperaments. Yet Nee taught many of us a greater appreciation of how Christ's death on the cross has given us the victory. For this alone the name of Watchman Nee is worthy of double honor (1 Tim. 5:17).

What Do I Think? A Personal, Emotional Assessment

In early part of 2005, I was asked to write a revised edition of my book *Understanding Watchman Nee.* I thought it wise because things had changed since I wrote that book 25 years ago. I am older now. I had lived in China. I had made a few more mistakes—committed sins that I am not proud of. I have been enriched in many more ways than I deserve. I thought it fair to be faithful to God and to be thankful for a man who preached the Gospel to many.

I prayed to God what I should say. I had mixed feelings. When I read again *The Normal Christian Life,* I again saw Nee's greatness. But as I read some of the letters and ideas in Witness Lee's biography, I saw a man too critical of others, but unable to accept criticism. Here's man who could write of faith in Christ so well and yet cried before God if people didn't agree with him. When millions around him were suffering poverty, famine, and torture under Japanese rule, Nee thought sharing in Christ's suffering was having church members disagree with you theologically. Getting stoned before an angry mob is suffering . Giving your last meal to a hungry family is closer to the "the fellowship of His sufferings" (Phil. 3:10) than having Christian disagreement. God gives us grace moments from people who are not Saints with a capital "S." There are just not enough of them to go around. We have to be happy with human ministers.

I don't know if Watchman Nee was the most mature, spiritual believer of the 20th century, as some would think. Thank God I am not psychic. I can't read Nee's mind. I didn't see everything he did. Only God can read our thoughts. First Corinthians makes it clear that we are not to proclaim ourselves followers of any single man, save the great God and Savior Jesus Christ. Paul regards such thinking as soulical or carnal. It is looking to man and not grace to save. Grace comes through the Word ministered by Paul, Apollos, Watchman Nee, C. S. Lewis, and any minister of the grace of Jesus Christ.

Over the years, I have met many people who are avid readers of Watchman Nee. They fall into two categories: 1) They love God and want to know more about the one they love; 2) They love God and want to be right at all times. Neither group has much trouble getting close to Jesus. It's accepting His body that's the bother.

The forty-fifth birthday is an important event. I know it is important for Canadians and Americans … more important than your twenty-first. Younger than forty-five and you think more of what you will do. After that birthday, you think about more about what you did. I am over forty-five and have dreams of my past fortunes. I remember Gus and Dot, two senior Baptists who have a real warmth and love for everyone. There were Joe and Wanda Hicks, my Pentecostal neighbors at graduate school. They were real Appalachians, the kind you would expect to be simple believers. In Boston, we'd call them "hicks." Yet, I never met a man so interested in understanding the Gospels in the original Greek and in the culture of Jesus' day. Wanda's greatest gift was laughter and hospitality with a big smile. Joe's was all the passion and friendship behind his favorite phrase, "Well, bless your heart." Then there were Don and Genevieve, Ken and Pat Seigel, Cliff and Fumiko, Don and Trudy, Laney Howe and Billy Graham. Some of them are gone; some live far away. There have just been so many great saints who showed that the Word became flesh. My daughters Rebecca and Jennifer and my son Andrew have taught lessons and shown me moments of grace that I think about every day. They all revealed Christ not by knowing a bigger list of revealed truths, but by being my children and my friends, and living as members of that great fellowship of the church, the Body of Christ.

I can't say if any of them ever knew as much as Watchman Nee did about the Bible. Yet there is one person I am certain who knows more about God's love and forgiveness. Her name is Mrs. Alpha Robertson. On Sunday morning, September 15, 1963 her thirteen-year-old daughter Carole rushed to the 16th Baptist Church in Birmingham, Alabama. It was Youth Sunday. She and her three friends, Cynthia Wesley, Denise McNair, and Addie May Collins, were eager to serve God.

I was nearly fifteen the day they died. I think it was the first time I cried for any stranger.

There was an explosion. In moments, they were all dead. Next to Carole's shattered frame was her purse. In Carole's purse was a Bible. For the next forty years, Alpha lives and teaches forgiveness. You can hear it in the way her voice trembles. You see it in her smile when she admits it's not that easy to forgive. The tears have not left her; neither the joy.[2]

When Watchman Nee went to prison, he was over forty-five years old. He could not write or compose his thoughts into teaching lessons. It was against prison regulations. He could only contemplate the blessings of Jesus Christ in his life and look forward to seeing Jesus face to face together with all the saints.

Chapter 6 Endnotes

1. Nee, *Spiritual Man*, 1:11.

2. 4 Little Girls. Dir. Spike Lee. DVD. Prod. 40 Acres and a Mule Filmworks and HBO Documentary Film. 1998.

Appendix A

Apology of A. Donald Fredlund and James Mo-Oi Cheung

April 19, 1973

TO WHOM IT MAY CONCERN:

Following publication of the book THE ECCLESIOLOGY OF WATCHMAN NEE AND WITNESS LEE by James Mo-Oi Cheung, we received personal visits and letters from associates of Witness Lee who asserted that he does not hold or teach some of the views that were attributed to him in the book. Accordingly, C.L.C. [Christian Literature Crusade] as publisher has taken the following actions:

1) Eight days after the book was first offered for sale, we removed the appendix in toto and rebound the remaining stock because of material in the appendix that we could not substantiate in light of the new information.

2) In mid-February we stopped all further sale of the book when it was brought to our attention that material which we could not substantiate was present in the body of the book as well.

3) We wrote a letter of apology to Mr. Witness Lee regarding imputations of heresy, etc., that the book contained.

4) We suspended publication of a revised and corrected edition of the book.

5) We issued a recall, for full credit, of all copies of the book sold.

6) We agreed that C.L.C. would not publish a revised edition of the book.

We feel that we owe to all parties interested in this publication a fuller explanation of the reasons for the actions detailed above. The following statement is intended to be the vehicle by which the author and publisher acknowledge that items in the areas mentioned below should not, for lack of supporting evidence, have appeared in the book. At the same time we do not mean to suggest that all believers would agree to all the teachings of Witness Lee and his associates.

Assertions by associates of Witness Lee that the book misrepresents him with respect to doctrine fall in these general areas:

1) Imputations of heresy to Witness Lee specifically in reference to his views on the blood of Jesus and the person and nature of Jesus Christ.

2) The claim that in matters of doctrine Witness Lee differs substantially from the views held by Watchman Nee (differences are evidently much narrower than suggested by the book).

3) The inference that Witness Lee resorts to deliberate "twisting of Scripture" or "misuse of the Word."

4) The allegation that Witness Lee holds to a strict "baptismal regeneration" view of baptism.

In addition, the authorship of the book THE GLORIOUS CHURCH was incorrectly attributed to Witness Lee, whereas the author was in fact Watchman Nee. We want it to be known that it is not our policy to disseminate material concerning any person or persons that is known to be inaccurate.

We sincerely regret feelings of offense created by the publication of this book, as well as any inconvenience caused by its subsequent recall and termination.

Sincerely in Christ,

CHRISTIAN LITERATURE CRUSADE

A. Donald Fredlund   James Mo-Oi Chc'ung

Publications Secretary   Author

Appendix B

On The Spiritual Man.
Fourth Editorial of Revival Magazine, April 3, 1952

[The following editorial is recorded in C.T. Chan's *My Uncle Watchman Nee*, pp. 118-120. It appears here for the first time in English, translated by Miss Joyce Leung and Mr. Wing-Tai Leung.]

The revised edition of *The Spiritual Man* has been sent to the publisher. The book was received very well. Those who just read the book, but have not received God as Savior, are going against the truth of the book.

During the past two years, there has been a revival in the church everywhere. That's God's power at work. But partly that is nature, supernature, at work too, not totally spiritual. The aim of *The Spiritual Man* is to point out the two themes to make people understand what is bad naturally; what is bad supernaturally; what is spiritual; and what is a bad influence. Those who have accepted Christ and the cross will have no problem distinguishing them.

Dramatic work and spiritual work can't be mixed. The flesh enjoys dramatic work, because it stimulates one's emotions. So, when one first sees truth he accepts it, but that doesn't mean that the truth is his. He has to pay for it. Many times the payment is agony in feeling. And many fail because they can't do it.

I am not against supernatural things. The Bible records many precious strange miracles. And I am not against people seeking for miracles; in fact, I encourage people to do so. But I would like to distinguish between miracles and the spiritual life. The former is not as precious as the latter. Besides, supernatural miracles can come from God or from the Devil (false spiritual work). So, I would like to find out their differences from the Bible so everybody can differentiate them.

A passive commission and an empty mind are very dangerous. I hope the readers of *The Spiritual Man* can really understand it and avoid these pitfalls.

Most people ask me about the dates of the revised edition. We cannot tell or fix it yet. Maybe after, we hope the brothers will be united in heart and spirit, lest there be errors.

The servant of the Family of Christ

Watchman Nee

Bibliography

[**Author's Note:** Living Stream Ministry has performed an admirable service to the study of Watchman Nee by making their translations of Nee's works available online.

Of course, printed versions are still valuable and available. You can't connect on a jet. It is hard to leisurely read a book carrying a laptop, extra batteries and praying that your wireless Internet service is there in a rustic Appalachian setting. In China online books are more practical. Christian books sometimes gets "lost" in the mail.

Online publications are more up-to-date than their printed counterparts. I have generally used the online publications copyright date.]

Assembly Together. Basic Lessons Series, vol. 3. [Translated by Stephen Kaung.] New York: Christian Fellowship Publishers, Inc., 1973.

Aids to "Revelation." [Translated by Stephen Kaung.] New York: Christian Fellowship Publishers, Inc., 1983.

The Assembly Life & The Prayer Ministry of the Church. Anaheim, Ca: Living Stream Ministry, 1997-2005. http://www.minstrybooks.org/collected-works.html.

Authority and Submission. Second Ed. Los Angeles: Living Stream Ministry, 1993.

Back to the Cross. New York: Christian Fellowship Publishers, Inc., 1983.

A Balanced Christian Life. [Translated by Stephen Kaung.] New York: Christian Fellowship Publishers, Inc., 1981.

Better Covenant. [Translated by Stephen Kaung.] New York:

Christian Fellowship Publishers, Inc., 1994.

The Body of Christ. Los Angeles: The Stream Publishers, n.d. [booklet].

The Body of Christ: A Reality. New York Christian Fellowship Publishers, 1978.

The Breaking of the Outer Man and the Release of the Spirit. Anaheim, Ca: Living Stream Ministry, 1997-2005. http://www.minstrybooks.org/collected-works.html.

Burden and Prayer. Taiwan: The Stream, n.d. [booklet].

Central Messages. Anaheim, Ca: Living Stream Ministry, 1997-2005. http://www.minstrybooks.org/collected-works.html.

The Character of God's Workman. New York: Christian Fellowship Publishers, Inc., 1988.

The Character of the Lord's Worker. Anaheim, Ca: Living Stream Ministry, 1997-2005. http://www.minstrybooks.org/collected-works.html.

Changed into His Likeness. Fort Washington, Pa.: Christian Literature Crusade.

Christ: The Sum of All Spiritual Things. [Translated by Stephen Kaung.] New York: Christian Fellowship Publishers, 1973.

The Christian. 5 Vol. Anaheim, Ca: Living Stream Ministry, 1997-2005. http://www.minstrybooks.org/collected-works.html.

The Christian (1930-1940). Anaheim, Ca: Living Stream Ministry, 1997-2005. http://www.minstrybooks.org/collected-works.html.

The Christian Life and Warfare. Anaheim, Ca: Living Stream Ministry, 1997-2005. http://www.minstrybooks.org/collected-works.html.

The Church and the Work.. New York: Christian Fellowship Publishers, Inc., 1982.

Collection of Newsletters. 2 vols. Anaheim, Ca: Living Stream Ministry, 1997-2005. http://www.minstrybooks.org/collected-works.html.

Church Affairs. Anaheim, Ca: Living Stream Ministry, 1997-2005. http://www.minstrybooks.org/collected-works.html.

Come, Lord Jesus. New York: Christian Fellowship Publishers, 1976.

Conferences, Messages, and Fellowship. 6 vols. Anaheim, Ca: Living Stream Ministry, 1997-2005. http://www.minstrybooks.org/collected-works.html.

Do All to the Glory of God. Basic Lesson Series, vol. 5. New York: Christian Fellowship Publishers, 1974.

The Finest of Wheat. 2 vols. New York: Christian Fellowship Publishers, Inc., 1993.

Full of Grace and Truth. 2 vols. New York: Christian Fellowship Publishers, 1981.

From Glory to Glory. New York: Christian Fellowship Publishers, 1985.

Further Talks on the Church Life. Taipei: The Gospel Book Room, 1968.

General Messages. 2 vols. Anaheim, Ca: Living Stream Ministry, 1997-2005. http://www.minstrybooks.org/collected-works.html.

The Glorious Church. Taipei: The Gospel Book Room, 1968.

The Glory of His Life. New York: Christian Fellowship Publishers, 1976.

The God of Abraham, Isaac, and Jacob. Anaheim, Ca: Living Stream Ministry, 1997-2005. http://www.minstrybooks.org/collected-works.html.

God's Plan and the Overcomers. New York: Christian Fellow-ship Publishers, 1977.

God's Work. New York: Christian Fellowship Publishers, Inc., 1974.

The Good Confession. Basic Lesson Series, vol. 2. [Translated by Stephen Kaung.] New York: Christian Fellowship Publishers, Inc., 1973.

Gospel Dialogue. New York: Christian Fellowship Publishers, 1975.

The Gospel of God. 2 vols. Anaheim, Ca: Living Stream Ministry, 1997-2005. http://www.minstrybooks.org/collected-works.html.

How to Study the Bible. Anaheim, Ca: Living Stream Ministry, 1997-

2005. http://www.minstrybooks.org/collected-works.html.

The King and The Kingdom of Heaven. New York: Christian Fellowship Publishers, Inc., 1978.

The Latent Power of the Soul. [Translated by Stephen Kaung.] New York: Christian Fellowship Publishers, Inc., 1972.

The Life That Wins. New York: Christian Fellowship Publishers, Inc., 1986.

A Living Sacrifice. Basic Lesson Series, vol. 1. [Translated by Stephen Kaung.] New York: Christian Fellowship Publishers, Inc., 1972.

Love Not the World. Edited by Angus I. Kinnear. Fort Washington, Pa.: Christian Literature Crusade, 1968.

Love One Another. Basic Lesson Series, vol. 6. [Translated by Stephen Kaung.] New York: Christian Fellowship Publishers, Inc., 1975.

Matured Leadings in the Lord's Recovery. 2 vols. Anaheim, Ca: Living Stream Ministry, 1997-2005. http://www.minstrybooks.org/collected-works.html.

Messages for Building Up New Believers. 3 vols. Anaheim, Ca: Living Stream Ministry, 1997-2005. http://www.minstrybooks.org/collected-works.html.

The Messenger of the Cross. New York: Christian Fellowship Publishers, 1980.

The Ministries & The Open Door. Anaheim, Ca: Living Stream Ministry, 1997-2005. http://www.minstrybooks.org/collected-works.html.

The Ministry of God's Word. [Translated by Stephen Kaung.] New York: Christian Fellowship Publishers, Inc., 1971.

Ministry to the House or to the Lord. Los Angeles: The Stream Publishers, n.d.

Miscellaneous Records of the Kuling Training. 2 vols. Anaheim, Ca: Living Stream Ministry, 1997-2005. http://www.minstrybooks.org/collected-works.html.

The *Mystery of Creation*. New York: Christian Fellowship Publishers, Inc., 1981.

The Normal Christian Church Life. Rev. ed. Washington: International Students Press, 1969.

The Normal Christian Church Life. Anaheim, Ca: Living Stream Ministry, 1997-2005. http://www.minstrybooks.org/collected-works.html.

The Normal Christian Life. Edited by Angus Kinnear. 3rd ed. Fort Washington, Pa.: Christian Literature Crusade, 1961.

The Normal Christian Faith. Anaheim, Ca: Living Stream Ministry, 1997-2005. http://www.minstrybooks.org/collected-works.html.

The Normal Christian Worker. Hong Kong: Hong Kong Church Book Room, 1965.

Not I, But Christ. Basic Lesson Series, vol. 4. [Translated by Stephen Kaung.] New York: Christian Fellowship Publishers, Inc., 1974.

Notes on Scriptural Message.3 vols. Anaheim, Ca: Living Stream Ministry, 1997-2005. http://www.minstrybooks.org/collected-works.html.

The Open Door. 2 vols. Anaheim, Ca: Living Stream Ministry, 1997-2005. http://www.minstrybooks.org/collected-works.html.

The Open Door & The Present Testimony. Anaheim, Ca: Living Stream Ministry, 1997-2005. http://www.minstrybooks.org/collected-works.html.

The Orthodoxy of the Church. Los Angeles: The Stream Publishers, 1970.

The Overcoming Life. Anaheim, Ca: Living Stream Ministry, 1997-2005. http://www.minstrybooks.org/collected-works.html.

Practical Issues of This Life. New York: Christian Fellowship Publishers, 1975.

The Prayer Ministry of the Church. [Translated by Stephen Kaung.] New York: Christian Fellowship Publishers, Inc., 1973.

The Present Testimony. 4 Vol. Anaheim, Ca: Living Stream Ministry, 1997-2005. http://www.minstrybooks.org/collected-works.html.

Questions on the Gospel Anaheim, Ca: Living Stream Ministry, 1997-2005. http://www.minstrybooks.org/collected-works.html.

The Release of the Spirit. Indianapolis: Premium Literature Co., 1965.

The Resumption of Watchman Nee's Ministry. Anaheim, Ca: Living Stream Ministry, 1997-2005. http://www.minstrybooks.org/collected-works.html.

The Salvation of the Soul. New York: Christian Fellowship Publishers, 1978.

Sit, Walk, Stand. 4th ed., rev. Fort Washington, Pa.: Christian Literature Crusade, 1962.

Song of Songs. Translated by Elizabeth K. Mei and Daniel Smith. Fort Washington, Pa.: Christian Literature Crusade, 1965.

The Song of Songs & Hymns. Anaheim, Ca: Living Stream Ministry, 1997-2005. http://www.minstrybooks.org/collected-works.html.

Spiritual Authority. [Translated by Stephen Kaung.] New York: Christian Fellowship Publishers, Inc., 1972.

Spiritual Judgment and Examples of Judgment. Anaheim, Ca: Living Stream Ministry, 1997-2005. http://www.minstrybooks.org/collected-works.html.

Spiritual Knowledge. [Translated by Stephen Kaung.] New York: Christian Fellowship Publishers, Inc., 1973.

The Spiritual Man. 3 vols. [Translated by Stephen Kaung.] New York: Christian Fellowship Publishers, Inc. 1968.

Spiritual Reality or Obsession. [Translated by Stephen Kaung.] New York: Christian Fellowship Publishers, Inc., 1970.

Study on Matthew. Anaheim, Ca: Living Stream Ministry, 1997-2005. http://www.minstrybooks.org/collected-works.html.

Study on Revelation. Anaheim, Ca: Living Stream Ministry, 1997-2005. http://www.minstrybooks.org/collected-works.html.

A Table in the Wilderness. Edited by Angus I. Kinnear. Fort Washington, Pa.: Christian Literature Crusade, 1965.

Take Head. New York: Christian Fellowship Publishers, Inc., 1991.

Twelve Baskets Full. 3 vols. Hong Kong: Hong Kong Church Book Room Ltd., 1965.

Twelve Baskets Full. Vol. 4. Hong Kong: Hong Kong Church Book Room, 1975.

The word of the Cross. Anaheim, Ca: Living Stream Ministry, 1997-2005. http://www.minstrybooks.org/collected-works.html.

What Shall This Man Do? Edited by Angus I. Kinnear. Fort Washington, Pa.: Christian Literature Crusade, 1961.

Ye Search the Scriptures. [Translated by Stephen Kaung.] New York: Christian Fellowship Publishers, Inc., 1974.

Watchman Nee's Testimony. Compiled by K.H. Weigh. Hong Kong: Church Book Room, 1974.

Watchman Nee's Testimony. Anaheim, Ca: Living Stream Ministry, 1997-2005. http://www.minstrybooks.org/collected-works.html.

Works on Watchman Nee

Chan, Stephen C.T. *Wo Ti Kau Fu Ni To Sheng* [*My Uncle Watchman Nee*]. Hong Kong: Alliance Press, 1970.

Chen, James. *Meet Brother Nee*. Hong Kong: The Christian Publishers, 1976.

Cheung, James Mo-Oi. *The Ecclesiology of Watchman Nee and Witness Lee*. Fort Washington, Pa.: Christian Literature Crusade, 1972.

Erling, Bernard. "The Story of Watchman Nee." *Lutheran Quarterly* 28(May 1976):140-55.

Fisher, G. Richard. "Watching out for Watchman Nee." Personal Freedom Outreach, n.d.

Henry, Carl F.H. "Footnotes: Watchman Nee." *Christianity Today*, May 9, 1975, pp. 31-32.

Kang-Shui [pseud.]. "The Case of Fraud in the Church: The Name of God Should Not Be Blasphemed." *Nan Pei Chi* 27 (Aug. 16,1972):9-10.

Kinnear, Angus I. *The Story of Watchman Nee: Against the Tide*. Fort Washington, Pa.: Christian Literature Crusade, 1973.

Leung Ka-lun. Watchman Nee: His Early Life and Thought [Chinese]. Hong Kong: Graceful House Limited, 2005.

_____. Watchman Nee: His Glory and Dishonor [Chinese]. Revised and enlarged edition. Hong Kong: Graceful House Limited, 2004.

Lo-Shah [pseud.]. "From 'The Case of Fraud in the Church': To See the Conspiracy of the Church by the Secret Organization, Part One." *Nan Pei Chi 32* (January 16, 1973):37-39.

_____. " From 'The Case of Fraud in the Church': To See the Conspiracy of the Church by the Secret Organization, Part Two." *Nan Pei Chi 33* (February 16,1973):44-46.

_____. "From 'The Case of Fraud in the Church': To See the Conspiracy of the Church by the Secret Organization, Part Three." *Nan Pei Chi 34* (March 10, 1973):56-60.

Lyall, Leslie. *Three of China's Mighty Men.* London: Overseas Missionary Fellowship, 1973.

Sources Consulted: Books

Alford, Henry. *The Greek Testament: With a Critically Revised Text: A Digest of Various Readings: Marginal References to Verbal and Idiomatic Usage; Prolegomena: And a Critical and Exegetical Commentary.* 4 vols. Boston: Lee and Shepard, 1888.

Allen, Roland. *The Ministry of the Spirit: Selected Writings of Roland Allen.* Reprinted. Edited by David M. Paton. Grand Rapids: William B. Eerdmans Publishing Co., 1962.

_____. *Missionary Methods: St. Paul's or Ours?* Grand Rapids: William B. Eerdmans Publishing Co., 1962.

_____. *The Spontaneous Expansion of the Church.* Grand Rapids: William B. Eerdmans Publishing Co., 1962.

Barabas, Steven. *So Great Salvation: The History of the Keswick Convention.* London: Marshall, Morgan and Scott, 1952.

Bardstra, Andrew. *The Law and the Elements of the World: An Exegetical Study in Aspects of Paul's Teaching.* Grand Rapids:

William B. Eerdmans Publishing Co., 1964.

Barr, Pat. *To China with Love*. Garden City, New York: Doubleday & Co., 1973.

Barth, Karl. *Church Dogmatics*. 4 vols. Edited by G.W. Bromily and T.F. Torrance. Edinburgh: T. & T. Clark, 1936-62.

Berton, Pierre. *The Comfortable Pew*. Philadelphia: J.B. Lippencott Company, 1965.

Blanford, Carl E. *Chinese Churches in Thailand*. Bangkok: Suriyaban Publishers, n.d.

Bloesch, Donald. *The Evangelical Renaissance*. Grand Rapids: William B. Eerdmans Publishing Co., 1973.

Boyd, Forrest. *Instant Analysis: Confessions of a White House Correspondent*. Atlanta: John Knox Press, 1974.

Bugh, Richard C., Jr. *Religion in Communist China*. Nashville: Abington Press, 1970.

Bruner, Frederick Dale. *A Theology of the Holy Spirit*. Grand Rapids: William B. Eerdmans Publishing Co., 1970.

Butterworth, G.W., ed. *Origin On First Principles*. New York: Harper & Row, 1966.

Clennell, WJ. *The Historical Development of Religion in China*. New York: E.P. Dutton & Co., 1917.

China Yearbook 1965-66. Taipei: China Publishing Company, 1966.

Coad, F. Roy. *A History of the Brethren Movement*. Exeter: The Paternoster Press, 1968.

Coates, C.A. *An Outline of the Song of Solomon*. Kingston-on-Thames, England: Stow Hill Bible and Tract Depot, n.d.

Cohen, Paul A. *China and Christianity: The Missionary Movement and Growth of Chinese Antiforeignism, 1860-1870*. Harvard East Asian Series, no. 11. Cambridge: Harvard University Press, 1963.

Colson, F.H. and Whitaker, G.H. *Philo*. 10 vols. The Loeb Classical Library. Cambridge: Harvard University Press, 1929.

Cruvellier, John Marc Etienne. *L'Exégèse de Romains 7 et le*

Mouvement de Keswick. Amsterdam: Drukkerij Pasmans, 1961.

Danielou, Jean, S.J. *From Shadows to Reality: Studies in the Typology of the Fathers.* Translated by Dom Wulstan Hillerd. London: Burnes & Oates, 1960.

Darby, J.N. *The Collected Writings of J.N. Darby.* 32 vols. Edited by William Kelly. London: G. Morrish, 1867-83.

Delitzsch, Franz. *A System of Biblical Psychology.* Edinburgh: T. & T. Clark, 1967.

Domes, Jurgen. *The International Politics of China, 1949-1972.* Translated by Rudiger Machetzki. New York: Praeger Publishers, 1973.

Douglas, Rev. W.M. *Andrew Murray and His Message: One of God's Choice Saints.* New York: Fleming H. Revell Co., n.d.

Ebon, Martin. *Lin Piao: The Life and Writings of China's New Ruler.* New York: Stein and Day, 1970.

Enroth, Ronald M.; Ericson, Edward E., Jr. and Peters, C. Breckinridge. *The Jesus People: Old Time Religion in the Age of Aquarius.* Grand Rapids: William B. Eerdmans Publishing Co., 1972.

Evans, Eifion. *The Welsh Revival of 1904.* London: Evangelical Press, 1969.

Fenn, C.H. *The Five Thousand Dictionary.* Cambridge: Harvard University Press, 1963.

Forsyth, Sidney A. *An American Missionary Community in China, 1895-1905.* Harvard East Asian Monographs 43, Cambridge: East Asian Research Center, Harvard University, 1971.

Foster, Harry. *A Study Guide to Watchman Nee's "The Normal Christian Life."* Eastbourne, England: Victory Press, 1976.

Frankfort, H. and H.A.; Wilson, John H. and Jacobsen, Thorkild. *Before Philosophy: The Intellectual Adventure of Ancient Man.* Baltimore: Penguin Books, 1951.

Frodsham, Stanley H. *With Signs Following.* Springfield, Mo.: Gospel Publishing House, 1946.

Gelpi, Donald L. *Pentecostalism: A Theological Viewpoint.* New

York: Paulist Press, 1971.

Giles, Herbert A. *A Chinese Biographical Dictionary*. Reprinted. Taipei: Literature House, n.d.

Girard, Marcel, ed. *Nagel's Encyclopedia-Guide: China*. Geneva: Nagel Publications, 1968.

Goertz, Peter S. *"A History of the Chinese Indigenous Christian Church under the American Board in Fukien Province."* Ph.D. dissertation, Yale University, 1933.

Green, Michael. *I Believe in the Holy Spirit*. Grand Rapids: William B. Eerdmans Publishing Co., 1975.

Grubb, Violet M. *The Chinese Indigenous Church Movement*. London: World Dominion Press, n.d.

Grudem, Wayne. *Systematic Theology*.Grand Rapids: Zondervan Books, 1995.

Guyon, Madame. *Autobiography of Madame Guyon*. Chicago: Moody Press, n.d.

Harford, John Battersby and MacDonald, Frederick Charles. *Handley Carr Glyn Moule*. London: Hodeer & Stoughton, 1922.

Harris, H.M. "Indigenous Churches in China." Ph.D. dissertation, Southern Baptist Theological Seminary, 1927.

Harrison; Everett F., ed. *Baker's Dictionary of Theology*. Grand Rapids: Baker Book House, 1973.

Harrison, John A. *China Since 1800*. New York: Harbinger Book, Harcourt, Brace & World, 1967.

Heard, Rev. J.B. *The Tripartite Nature of Man*. Edinburgh: T. & T. Clark, 1875.

Henry, Carl F.H. *Christian Personal Ethics*. Grand Rapids: William B. Eerdmans Publishing Co. 1957.

Hollenweger, Walter J. *The Pentecostals: The Charismatic Movement in the Churches*. Translated by R.A. Wilson. Minneapolis: Augsburg Publishing House, 1972.

Hopkins, Evan H. *The Law of Liberty in the Spiritual Life*. Philadelphia: The Sunday School Times, 1952.

Isaacs, Harold R. *Images of Asia*. New York: Capricorn Books, 1962

Ivanhoe, Philip J. and Van Norden, Bryan W. *Readings in Classical Chinese Philosophy*. New York: Seven Bridges Press, 2001.

Jamieson, Robert; Fausset, A.R.; and Brown, David. *Commentary, Critical and Explanatory on the Old and New Testaments*. 2 vols. Hartford: S.S. Scranton and Co., 1887.

Jewett, Robert. *Paul's Anthropological Terms: A Study of Their Use in Conflict Settings*. Arbeiten zur Geschichte des Antiken Judentums and des Urchristentums. Band 10. Leiden: E. J. Brill, 1971.

Jones, Francis Price. *The Church in Communist China: A Protestant Appraisal*. New York: Friendship Press, 1962.

Jordon, David K. *Gods, Ghosts, and Ancestors: The Folk Religion of a Taiwanese Village*. Los Angeles: University of California Press, 1972.

Kaung, Stephen. *The Song of Degrees*. New York: Christian Fellowship Publishers, Inc., 1970.

_____. *The Splendor of His Ways: Seeing the Lord's End in Job*. New York: Christian Fellowship Publishers, 1974.

Keswick Convention Trustees. *The Keswick Convention 1938*. London: Pickering & Inglis, 1938.

_____. *The Keswick Week 1948*. London: Marshall, Morgan & Scott, 1948.

Kittel, Gerhard and Friedrich, Gerhard, eds. *Theological Dictionary of the New Testament*. 10 vols. translated by Geoffrey W. Bromiley. Grand Rapids: William B. Eerdmans Publishing Co. 1964-76.

Klein, Donald W. and Clark, Ann B. *Biographic Dictionary of Chinese Communism 1921-1965*. 2 vols. Cambridge: Harvard University Press, 1971.

Kummel, Werner Georg. *Romer 7 and Die Bekenhrung Des Paulus*. Leipzig: J.C. Hinrichs'sche Buchhandlung, 1929.

Ladd, George Eldon. *A Theology of the New Testament*. Grand Rapids: William B. Eerdmans Publishing Company, 1975.

Lane, William. *The Gospel According to Mark: The English Text with Introduction, Exposition and Notes.* The New International Commentary on the New Testament. Grand Rapids: William B. Eerdmans Publishing Company, 1974.

La Rondelle, Hans Karl. *Perfection and Perfectionism.* Amsterdam: J.H. Kok N.V. Kampen, 1971.

Latourette, Kenneth Scott. *The Chinese: Their History and Culture.* New York: Macmillan Co., 1962.

Lee, Witness. *The Baptism in the Holy Spirit.* Los Angeles: The Stream Publishers, 1969.

_____. *Christ vs. Religion.* Taipei: The Gospel Book Room, [1971].

_____. *The Economy of God,* Los Angeles: The Stream Publishers, 1968.

_____. *The Four Major Steps of Christ.* Los Angeles: The Stream Publishers, 1969.

_____. *The Parts of Man.* Los Angeles: The Stream Publishers, 1969.

Legge, James. *Christianity in China: Nestorianism, Roman Catholicism, Protestantism.* London: Trubner & Co., 1888.

Lyall, Leslie T. *Come Wind, Come Weather: The Present Experience of the Church in China.* Chicago: Moody Press, 1960.

_____. *Red Sky at Night: Communism Confronts Christianity in China.* Chicago: Moody Press, 1969.

McDonough, Mary E. *God's Plan of Redemption.* Boston: Hamilton Brothers, 1922.

_____. *The Story of Redemption.* Bournemouth, England: The "Overcomer" Bookroom, n.d.

Matthews, David. *I Saw the Welsh Revival.* Chicago: Moody Press, 1951.

Metcalfe, J.C. *In the Mould of the Cross: A Pen-Sketch of the Life and Ministry of Jessie Penn-Lewis.* Dorset, England: Overcomer Literature Trust, n.d.

Meyer, Heinrich August Wilhelm. *Critical and Exegetical Handbook to the Gospels of Mark and Luke*. Translated by Robert Ernest Wallis and William P. Dickson. Edinburgh: T. & T. Clark, 1883.

Michelson, A. Berkeley. *Interpreting the Bible*. Grand Rapids: William B. Eerdmans Publishing Co., 1963.

Minnear, Paul S. *Horizons of Christian Community*. St. Louis, Mo.: The Bethany Press, 1959.

Morgan, G. Campbell and Stead, W.T. *The Welsh Revival*. Boston: The Pilgrim Press, 1905.

Moule, Handley C.G. *Outline of Christian Doctrine*. London: Hodder & Stoughton, 1902.

Murray, Andrew. *The Spirit of Christ*. Fort Washington, Pa.: Christian Literature Crusade, 1963.

Murray, John. *The Epistle to the Romans, The New International Commentary on the New Testament*. Grand Rapids: William B. Eerdmans Publishing Co., 1968.

National Council of Churches of Christ in the U.S.A. *Documents of the Three-Self Movement: Source Materials for the Study of the Protestant Church in Communist China*. New York: Far Eastern Office, Division of Foreign Missions, 1963.

Newham, Richard. *About Chinese*. Baltimore: Penguin Books, 1971.

Niebuhr, Reinhold. *The Nature and Destiny of Man*. New York: Charles Scribner's Sons, 1949.

Pakenham-Welsh, W.S. *Twenty Years in China*. Cambridge: W. Heffer & Sons, 1935.

Palmer, Edwin H. *The Five Points of Calvinism*. Grand Rapids: Baker Book House, 1972.

_____. *The Person and Ministry of the Holy Spirit: The Traditional Calvinistic Perspective*. Grand Rapids: Baker Book House, 1974.

Paton, David M. *Christian Missions and the Judgment of God*. London: S.C.M. Press, 1953.

_____. ed. *Reform of the Ministry: A Study in the Work of Roland Allen*. London: Lutterworth Press, 1968.

Patterson, George N. *Christianity in Communist China*. Waco,

Texas: Word Books, 1969.

Paxson, Ruth. *Called unto Holiness.* Grand Rapids: Zondervan Publishing House, n.d.

————. *Life of the Highest Plane.* 3 vols. New York: Fleming H. Revell Co., 1928.

Pember, G.H. *Earth's Earliest Ages.* Old Tappan, N.J.: Fleming H. Revell Co., n.d.

Penn-Lewis, Jessie. *The Awakening in Wales.* Dorset, England: The Overcomer Literature Trust, n.d.

————. *The Centrality of the Cross.* Dorset, England: The Overcomer Literature Trust, n.d.

————. *The Cross of Calvary.* Dorset, England: The Overcomer Literature Trust, n.d.

————. *Life in the Spirit.* Dorset, England: The Overcomer Literature Trust, n.d.

————. *Life out of Death.* Dorset, England: The Overcomer Literature Trust, n.d.

————. *Soul and Spirit: A Glimpse into Bible Psychology.* Dorset England: The Overcomer Literature Trust, n.d.

————. *The Spiritual Warfare.* Dorset, England: The Overcomer Literature Trust, n.d.

————. *The Hidden Ones.* Dorset, England: The Overcomer Literature Trust, n.d.

————. and Roberts, Evan. *War on the Saints.* Dorset, England: The Overcomer Literature Trust, n.d.

Philip, Robert. *Peace with China! or, The Crisis of Christianity in Central Asia: A Letter to the Right Honourable T.B. Macauly, Secretary of War.* London: John Snow, 1840.

Pierson, Arthur T. *The Bible and Spiritual Criticism.* Reprint ed. Grand Rapids: Baker Book House, 1970.

————. *Forward Movements of the Last Half Century.* New York: Funk & Wagnalls Co., 1905.

Pierson, Delavan Leonard. *Arthur T. Pierson.* New York: Fleming H. Revell Co., 1912.

Pollock, John C. *The Keswick Story.* London: Hodeer & Stoughton, 1964.

Reid, William. *Plymouth Brethrenism: Unveiled and Refuted.* Edinburgh: William Oliphant & Co., 1880.

Ridderbos, Herman. *Paul: An Outline of His Theology.* Translated by Richard de Witt. Grand Rapids: William B. Eerdmans Publishing Co., 1975.

Robinson, H. Wheeler. *The Christian Doctrine of Man.* 3rd ed. Edinburgh: T. & T. Clark, 1926.

Sandeen, Ernest R. *The Origins of Fundamentalism.* Facet Books. Historical Series No. 10. Philadelphia: Fortress Press, 1968.

_____. *The Roots of Fundamentalism: British and American Millenarianism 1800-1930.* Chicago: The University of Chicago Press, 1968.

Schurmann, Franz. *Ideology and Organization in Communist China.* Enlarged ed. Berkeley: University of California Press, 1968.

Scofield, Rev. C.I., gen. ed., *The Scofield Reference Bible.* 2nd ed. New York: Oxford University Press, 1917.

Singh, Bakht. *God's Dwelling Place.* Bombay: Gospel Literature Service, 1957.

Smith, C. Ryder. *The Bible Doctrine of Grace.* London: The Epworth Press, 1956.

_____. *The Bible Doctrine of Man.* London: The Epworth Press, 1951.

Smith, Daniel. *Bakht Singh of India: A Prophet of God.* Washington: International Students Press, n.d.

Sparks, Jack. *The Mind Benders.* New York: Thomas Nelson Publishers, 1976.

Stevenson, Herbert F., *Keswick's Authentic Voice.* Grand Rapids: Zondervan Publishing House, 1959.

_____. , ed. *Keswick's Triumphal Voice.* Grand Rapids: Zondervan

Publishing House, 1963.

Stewart, James Livingstone. *Chinese Culture and Christianity*. New York: Fleming H. Revell Co., 1926.

Stoeffler, F. Earnest. *German Pietism During the Eighteenth Century*. Leiden: E. J. Brill, 1973.

_____. *The Rise of Evangelical Pietism*. Leiden: E.J. Brill, 1965.

Strachey, Ray. *Group Movements of the Past and Experiments in Guidance*. London: Faber & Faber, 1934.

Tierney, Lawrence M. and others, eds. *Current Medical Diagnosis & Treatment*. McGraw-Hill, 2000.

Torrey, R.A. *The Holy Spirit: Who He Is and What He Does*. New York: Fleming H. Revell Co., 1927.

Tregear, J.R. *A Geography of China*. Chicago: Aldine Publishing Co., 1965.

Tse-Shing, Tang [pseud.]. *Death Blow to Corrupt Doctrines: A Plain Statement of Facts*. Shanghai: The Gentry and People, 1870.

Underhill, Evelyn. *The Life of the Spirit and the Life of Today*. New York: E. P. Dutton & Co., 1922.

Walvoord, John F. *The Rapture Question*. Grand Rapids: Zondervan Publishing House, 1964.

Wang, Mary. *Stephen the Chinese Pastor*. London: Hodder & Stoughton, 1973.

Warfield, Benjamin Breckinridge. *Perfectionism*. Edited by Samuel G. Craig. Philadelphia: The Presbyterian and Reformed Publishing Co. 1971.

Watson, J.R. *The English Hymn: A Critical and Historical Study*, Oxford, England: Oxford University Press, 1999.

Wehrle, Edmund S. Britain, *China and the Anti-missionary Riots, 1891-1900*. Minneapolis: University of Minnesota Press, 1966.

Wesley, John. *Wesley's Standard Sermons*. 2 vols. Edited by Edward H. Sugden. Nashville: Lamar & Barton, n.d.

_____. *The Works of John Wesley*. 14 vols. Edited by Thomas

Jackson. Reprinted. Kansas City, Mo.: Nazarene Publishing House, n.d.

Williams, Edward Thomas. *A Short History of China*. New York: Harper & Brothers, 1928.

Wilson, Marvin R. *Our Father Abraham: Jewish roots of the Christian Faith*. Grand Rapids, MI: William B. Eerdmans, 1999.

Yamamoto, J. Isamu. *The Puppet Master*. Downers Grove, Ill.: Inter-Varsity Press, 1977.

Other Sources Consulted

Adeney, David. "The China Watch." *Christianity Today* 20 (November 21, 1975):10-12.

American Board of Missions. *Foochow Missionaries Documents*, 1846-54, 1860-80, 1920-29.

Balsama, George. "Madame Guyon, Heterodox." *Church History* 42 (1973): 350-65.

Cheung, James Mo-Oi and Fredlund, A. Donald. "To Whom It May Concern." Letter, Christian Literature Crusade, April 19, 1973.

China Bulletin. 1949-1980.

Crane, Burton. "Evangelist Drive Sweeps Formosa." *New York Times*, October 8, 1950, sec. 1. p. 11.

Fritsch, Charles T. "Biblical Typology." Bibliotheca Sacra 104 (1947):87-100, 214-22.

_____. "To Anti-Typon" in *Studia Biblica et Semitica*. Wageningen, Netherlands: H. Veeman en Zonen N.K., 1966. pp. 100-111.

Gasque, Ward. "The Biblical View of Man." Cassette recording, Vancouver, B.C.: Logos Tapes of Canada, n.d.

Hollenweger, Walter J. "Unusual Methods of Evangelism in the Pentecostal Movement in China." *A Monthly Letter about Evangelism* 8/9 (November/ December 1965):1-5.

Kaung, Stephen to Dana Roberts. November 13, 1972. Personal letter.

King, Harold G. "How I Kept Strong in Faith in a Chinese Communist Prison." *The Watchtower*, July 15, 1963, pp. 437-439.

The Stream. 1973-75.

" 'Little Flock' and Middle School Students." *Religious Education Fellowship, English Bulletin*, May 1937, pp. 33-34.

Living Stream Ministry. *LSM Hymn Collection* at http://witness-lee-hymns.org/lsm/index.html; Accessed May 24, 2005.

Lyall, Leslie. "Evangelization by Migration." *China's Millions* 58 (1950):170.

Markus, R.A. "Presuppositions of the Typological Approach to Scripture." In *The Communication of the Gospel in New Testament Times*, pp. 75-93, S.P.C.K. Theological Collections. London: S.P.C.K., 1961.

Murray, D.S. "The Building of the Church in Village Communities Twenty Years Experience in North China." *International Review of Missions* 7(1918):363-72.

Notson, Charles E. "Individualism Gone Astray: II. The 'Little Flock' of Watchman Ngnee." *The Alliance Weekly* November 12, 1952, pp. 729-30.

Pollock, John. "A Hundred Years of Keswick." *Christianity Today*, June 20, 1975, pp. 6-8.

Pryke, J. "'Spirit'and 'Flesh' in the Qumran Documents and Some New Testament Texts." *Revue De Qumran 5* (1965):345-60.

Rowley, H.H. "The Interpretation of the Song of Songs." *Journal of Theological Studies* 38 (1937):337-63.

Schmitt, Charles. *A Correction of the "Local Church Ground Teaching" as Held by Followers of Witness Lee*. Grand Rapids: Fellowship of Body of Christ, n.d. (pamphlet).

Spiritual Counterfeits Project. "Trip of the Month: Witness Lee and the Local Church." *Newsletter* 6 (July-August 1975).

Stearns, Mrs. Carol T. Church at Hollis, Hollis, New York. Interview,

October 14, 1972.

Stuart, Douglas. Gordon-Conwell Theological Seminary, S. Hamilton, Mass. Interview, October 10, 1974.

_____. "The Bible, Dualism, and Christian Good Works." *Inside*, November 1972, pp. 18-22.

Stube, The Rev. Edwin to Dana Roberts February 16, 1975. Personal letter.

The SPIRIT-FILLED CLASSICS Collection

Secrets of Watchman Nee is the latest addition to
the Bridge-Logos Spirit-Filled Classics Collection.

This inspiring collection includes biographies of famous men
and women who operated in the Gifts of the Spirit as well as
time-honored works by these influential figures.

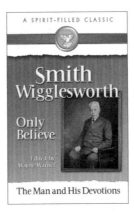

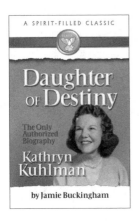

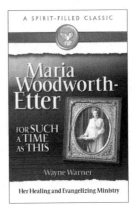

AVAILABLE AT FINE CHRISTIAN BOOKSTORES